Kingston upon Hull City l
WITHDRAWN
FROM STOCK
FOR SALE

AVE

ASPECTS OF FAITH

The History of Hull and District
Theological Society 1957-2007

by
Barbara M. Robinson

Highgate of Beverley

Highgate Publications (Beverley) Limited
2007

British Library Cataloguing in Publication Data.
A catalogue record for this book is available from the British Library.

© 2007 Barbara M. Robinson

Barbara Robinson asserts the moral right to be identified as the author of this work.

ISBN 9781 902645 48 3

Highgate of Beverley
Highgate Publications (Beverley) Limited
24 Wylies Road, Beverley, HU17 7AP. Telephone (01482) 866826

Produced by Highgate Print Limited
24 Wylies Road, Beverley, HU17 7AP. Telephone (01482) 866826

HULL LIBRARIES	
01276513/	
Bertrams	16.01.08
230.06	£7.50
AVE 2\08	

Contents

Foreword by The Bishop of Hull iv

Presidents – Past and Present v

The Hull and District Theological Society in Context
   by Dr David Bagchi 1

On The Record – The First Decade 10

The Second Decade 33

The Third Decade 44

The Fourth Decade 56

The Fifth Decade 71

Index 111

Foreword
by The Bishop of Hull

Congratulations to the Hull and District Theological Society on its Golden Jubilee!

I shall always remember the former Prime Minister, Harold Wilson, dismissing things which he thought were of no practical use as 'just theology'.

On the contrary, there is no more important subject in the world. How timely it is that the Jubilee of the Hull and District Theological Society coincides with the anniversary of the Abolition of the Slave Trade – a classic example of theological beliefs emanating in practical action.

The list of past patrons, presidents, and honorary members of the Society is impressive indeed. My hope is that the Society will go from strength to strength: uniting the theory and the practice of theology is to be commended and encouraged.

Richard Frith
Bishop of Hull

Presidents Past and Present

The Founder President of the Society, the Revd. E. J. Tinsley, 1957-1962, Bishop of Bristol, 1976-1985. Picture by permission of the Dean and Chapter of Bristol Cathedral.

The Revd. Professor Anthony Hanson, left, President of the Society from 1962 to 1982, receiving a presentation to mark his 70th birthday from his successor, the Revd. I. P. Ellis (1983 to 1987). The gift was a bound copy of Scripture: Meaning and Method, *a collection of essays by a number of scholars, including former external examiners to the Department of Theology and past and present members of staff.*

Dr Wendy Sproston North (1987 to 1991) and Dr J. Lionel North (1993 to 1997)

Prof. L. L. Grabbe (1991 – 1993) left, and Dr David Bagchi (1997 –).

The Hull and District Theological Society in Context

By Dr David Bagchi, MA., DPhil (Oxon), FRHistS

Going merely by appearances, the casual visitor might assume that Hull and its surrounding district is an obvious location for a local theological society. Its principal church, Holy Trinity – the largest parish church in England by area – and the famous Minster in nearby Beverley testify to the vitality of its religious culture. The striking equestrian statue of William of Orange in the Market Place and the imposing monument to the Evangelical social reformer William Wilberforce in Queens Gardens are clues to the later Protestantism of the city of Hull itself. And a dedicated educational quarter a couple of miles north of the city centre was until recently home to not one but two universities.

But appearances can deceive. The region has so little interest in religion that it has one of the lowest rates of church attendance in England, and as for education, the city's secondary schools consistently foot the national league tables – not the most fruitful conditions for the establishment of a society devoted to the promotion of 'the study of theology in all its branches'. But, as Barbara Robinson's account shows, such a society was established, and rather against the odds has survived the vicissitudes of fifty years. The purpose of this chapter is to fill out some of the theological and academic background to Secretary Robinson's account, with reference both to national and to local factors.

The formation of the Society

Let us begin at the beginning, with that meeting one winter's evening in 1956, in the University's Senior Common Room. This was located in what is today the Cohen Building, one of a pair of squarish, redbrick, neo-Elizabethan-looking buildings that were the first permanent structures on the campus. At this time the University consisted of just four buildings proper supplemented by a collection of Nissen huts; the rest of the campus was literally that, a field. But plans were in hand for a massive programme of works that over the next ten years would transform the site into something approaching the campus we know today, and expectancy of great things was in the air. Moreover, the University had received its royal charter from the young Queen barely two years before, and one can imagine the optimism with which our pioneering New Elizabethans made their way through the darkness to the Science and Social Building.[1]

The twenty-one people who gathered that evening were agreed on what had drawn them: the success of the day schools organized by the Hull Council of Churches and the University's Adult Education Department, the growing number of extra-mural classes in Theology, and a general revival of interest in theological matters. This upsurge of interest was described in the following words by someone who was probably present at that meeting:

> 'Inside the Churches very many laymen are wanting to enlarge and clarify their grasp of the Faith, to lift it to an adult and really educated level, either for this good end alone or because they may be needed (as many certainly are) to lend a hand in the Churches' teaching function, as lay readers, lay preachers, leaders of discussion groups, and so on . . .
>
> Outside the Churches there is a large body of people searching for a view of the world and a way of life who realise that they cannot go far without facing religious questions.'[2]

The mid-1950s was indeed an auspicious time for such a venture. There had been a war; and the loss, privation, sacrifice, and heroism that had inspired had shown to many the reality of the transcendent in this life, and had inspired many to seek the things that make for lasting peace. The Ecumenical Movement and the Liturgical Movement of the earlier twentieth century had re-focussed attention on what united Christians – the Bible and the early Church Fathers – and research in these areas was already resulting in encouraging progress on hitherto intractable problems. And the 'Higher Criticism' of the Bible that had seemed so corrosive of Christian belief for much of the century was now inspiring 'Biblical Theology', a constructive theology which embraced the assured results of Biblical criticism.

The restoration of Scripture as the foundation of Christian belief and action was in part a result of the neo-orthodox turn represented by Karl Barth: not only did it seem that theologians were now actually helping support the faith of ordinary church-goers rather than undermining it but also (in the case of anti-Nazi heroes such as Dietrich Bonhoeffer, Martin Niemöller, and Barth himself) showing that a theologically-informed Christianity was an antidote – perhaps the antidote – to the totalitarian tyrannies of the twentieth century. (One might venture the romantic thought that this association of Protestantism and freedom would have appealed strongly to the self-image of a city which had defied one king, reviled as a Catholic tyrant, and which had set up a golden statue to another, who had guaranteed Protestant liberties after the Revolution, and of course to a city whose most famous son was an Evangelical who had promoted the abolition of the slave trade.)

The power of the state, the growing influence of consumerist culture, and the always imminent prospect of nuclear annihilation were also at this time focussing attention on Christian re-workings of existentialist philosophy. Paul Tillich, who was a thoroughly Americanized German academic (and like all things American quite irresistible to drab, 1950s Britain), showed that fashionable *rive-gauche* ideas of 'alienation' and 'being' were simply new ways of talking about sin and everlasting life.

'Media dons' were emerging as an identifiable species, and some of their ideas were being popularized on the wireless, through the BBC's Third Programme, as well as in affordable paperbacks. An appetite was created, but (then as now) few preachers would have been willing to discuss academic theology from the pulpit for fear of disturbing the weaker brethren. Now the people of Hull had their own university, and it seemed only right that it should help bring theological light to the region, in fulfilment of its proud motto.[3]

The general upsurge of interest in theology at this time was well enough known. But a specific factor was identified at the meeting; the success of the day schools and the Theology classes put on by the Adult Education department. One way in which Hull differed from both ancient and modern universities was in the relative size and importance of its extra-mural department: when the university college opened in 1928, Adult Education was the largest department.[4] In fact, until the early 1990s, when the subject staff of Adult Education were formally re-assigned to the academic schools, many departments (Theology among them) were able to teach the numbers of full-time students they did only by relying on the help of adult education staff.

The geographical reach of the Adult Education department was considerable, spanning both sides of the Humber and making significant inroads into the North Riding of Yorkshire and into Lincolnshire, as well as of course as the East Riding.[5] This perhaps explains why 'The Theological Society of Hull and District', to give it its official pre-1999 name, was not entitled simply 'the Hull Theological Society'. That would have disenfranchized many proudly independent non-Hullites. It perhaps also explains why the rules of the Society stipulated that 'one meeting in each year will be held outside the city of Hull'. This stipulation has never been honoured in the observance, so far as one can see, and the apodictic 'will' has over the years been downgraded to a concessive 'may'. But no matter: the clause is there and an important principle is established.

At any rate, the rules of the Society agreed the following year guaranteed one committee place to a member of the Department of Adult Education staff. Significantly also, the head of the department, Professor G.E.T. Mayfield, was the first non-archiepiscopal recipient of an honorary membership of the Society.

While Adult Education was a long-established feature of University

College, Hull, the Department of Theology was one of several new departments that had come into being only in 1954, when UCH became a university. Theology of a sort – the religious and moral instruction sort – had been taught at UCH since before the Second World War. In common with all universities and university colleges before the raising of the age of majority in 1970, UCH was *in loco parentis* for its students under the age of 21, and it had the obligations of a parent with respect to the moral guidance of most of the undergraduates in its care. Appropriate instruction included lectures in the principles of Christian doctrine and ethics, and these were given by Thomas Edmund Jessop. Jessop, who had been Ferens Professor of Philosophy at UCH since its foundation in 1928, was principally a philosopher with a particular interest in George Berkeley, but was widely known for his wartime pamphlets and broadcasts for servicemen on religious matters. He was made the second honorary member of the Society.[6] The lectures were arranged through the University's Religious Activities Committee, which in this sense can claim to have fathered the Theology Department proper. And with the formation of a dedicated department, Theology was offered as a full degree.

When the 1956 meeting agreed to form a theological society 'based on the University in close relation to its Theological Department', the mutual benefits would have been obvious. The Department would provide leadership of the Society and confer academic respectability upon it. The Society would give the young department what would nowadays be called a capacity for 'reach-out into the community'. To this day, it affords the Theology unit a local and regional profile which few other academic departments can boast.[7]

Having sketched in the wider intellectual background and the role of the University at the time of the Society's inception, it remains only to consider the significance of the local theological society as a nationwide trend at the time of the Society's inception. Not counting exclusively 'gown' affairs such as Cambridge Theological Society, by 1956 local societies had already been established at Bristol, Newcastle upon Tyne, and Norwich, and there may have been others. But the Hull records make no reference whatever to any knowledge of their existence. No-one thought to follow the examples of others in drafting a constitution, in deciding upon the nature, duration, and frequency of talks, or even in setting conditions of membership or the level of subscriptions. If they did, no-one recorded the fact. Rather, the opening clause of the 1957 *Rules* declares grandly that '[f]or all but legal purposes it shall be known as The Theological Society', as if it were quite *sui generis*.

This situation was not at all unusual among theological societies in Britain. The only other history of a society is that for Leicester's, founded in 1958 and with many of the same features as Hull's, not least the association with a place of learning (in Leicester's case, Vaughan's College, later incorporated into the University of Leicester), and the mixture of local and visiting speakers. But there is no mention of the HDTS or of any other society for that matter in the account of the society's genesis. Unlike the network of local branches of the Historical Association or the Classical Association, there is no national co-ordinating body. This means that theological societies lack several advantages, including access to subvention from the national bodies to defray the travelling costs of speakers, and access to a national database of speakers and the subjects on which they would be willing to speak.

Such autonomy also has its advantages, however, as the example of the almost exactly contemporary William Temple Association demonstrates. Founded in 1955 as a national body charged with establishing local branches throughout the country, its purpose initially was to activate professional and graduate Anglican laymen in the service of the social gospel, through regular meetings for training and mutual support – an Anglican version of the Rotarians, in effect. The distinctions based on sex and class were soon dropped (though the ban on clergy remained), and meetings began to concentrate on issues of general theological interest. The local branches became local theological societies in all but name. However, the dissolution of the national association in 1984 led to the dissolution of the majority of local branches as well, so that now only four survive.[8]

The progress of the Society

The Society is fortunate in having had a succession of conscientious secretaries who have preserved its records so completely. But it is sad to report that, until 1998, no records were kept of the content of any of the papers given, which after all were the Society's *raison d'être*. There are no transcripts, no tapes, not even any summaries or notes. Of course, in the case of speakers who were also published authors, one can have a fair stab at reconstructing what they must have said at the time they spoke to the Society; but it is frustrating not to know exactly. It would also be very illuminating to know what happened in the question-and-answer sessions that followed. The minutes of the AGMs simply tell us that the papers were well-received or greatly appreciated by all concerned. That was no doubt the case. All who attended were evidently very interested in the topic, and the speakers were all of proven calibre; but it is regrettable that we cannot get behind this rather formulaic minute.

The speakers include, as it was always intended they should, the most famous UK-based theologians from each decade (although the 'Professor C. H. Dodd' who spoke in 1981 was not the biblical scholar!). In addition, they include members of the Theology department and of other departments in the University, most addressing issues of professional interest to them, others revealing an amateur but well-informed theological hobby. Local clergy are well represented among the speakers, as are

Theology students from the University. 'Student evenings' were devoted to short papers by undergraduates who were pursuing a special interest sparked by one of the courses they were doing. Professor Eamon Duffy, one of the foremost church historians of our day, cut his academic teeth by contributing to such an evening. From 2000, similar evenings were put on instead for graduate students in Theology, who in many cases could claim credits towards their research training programmes for having delivered and defended their ideas in public.

The shift in the nature of the student evening is interesting, not least because it reflects the fact that, with the substitution of loans for maintenance grants, most full-time undergraduates at Hull today are obliged to undertake paid employment during term-time, in order to keep within bounds the debt they will incur by the time they graduate (£13,000 per graduate, on average). Often taking jobs serving in bars or waiting in restaurants, they are unable to attend evening meetings and lack the time to write papers for which they receive no direct academic credit. Members benefit from hearing perhaps more accomplished work, and more polished performances, from research students; but it is undoubtedly a loss overall to the life of the Society that undergraduates are effectively excluded from it.

Despite the range of papers delivered over the years there is, however, the loud silence of a dog not barking – a brace of dogs, in fact. The reader will scan the annual programmes of the HDTS in vain for evidence of the impact of the two most notorious theological *causes célèbres* of the late twentieth century, the 'Honest to God' controversy sparked by a book of the same name by Bishop John Robinson in the early 1960s, and the 'myth of God incarnate' controversy of the late 1970s, occasioned by a collection of essays under that title edited by Dennis Nineham. These absences are quite astonishing. The exception is the paper given in 1978 by the Lady Margaret Professor of Divinity at Oxford University, John Macquarrie, who had contributed to a riposte to Nineham's book entitled *The Truth of God Incarnate*. But this merely proves the rule, for the advertised subject of his talk was not christology but non-Christian religions.

We should, however, again be aware of the limitation of our sources. As we do not have any records of the papers given, we do not know that such issues were *not* addressed, either in the course of the paper itself or in the questions afterwards. (In Macquarrie's case, for instance, it is obvious that his advertised title could have provided great scope for considering the question of the uniqueness of Christianity, and therefore have been entirely topical.) Moreover, it would be possible for a speaker to change his or her title completely on the day, and for this fact not to have been recorded. It should also be borne in mind that the Society was not the only, or even necessarily the best, forum for exploring such debates. The day schools provided opportunities for the discussion of topical subjects that involved more than one speaker, and that was therefore representative of different viewpoints.

Over the decades we see the nature of the relationship between the Society and its surroundings change and adapt, and some of the original principles of the founders erode with the passage of time and the change of personnel. One of these we have already encountered, the stipulation in the *Rules* that one meeting a year be held outside the city of Hull. The records show that the Society met somewhere other than the University only twice, in 1958 and 1981, when it assembled at the Hull Municipal Training College (later Hull College of Higher Education) – literally next door to the University! The attractions of a regular venue that was (usually) available free of charge and that (usually) offered plentiful parking spaces were simply too great.

Another departure from the *Rules* took place in 1987, on the retirement of the Revd Ieuan Ellis. Up until this time, the head of the Theology department had been president of the Society *ex officio*. This arrangement ensured that the Society was, if not central, at least proximate to the life of the department. But it also entailed an additional, if small, administrative burden on an office that was becoming increasingly complex and bureaucratic, and which in the case of Theology after 1982 was increasingly concerned with the vital question of the department's survival. The advantages of deputing the leadership of the Society to a staff member who could devote more time to it must have over-ridden constitutional considerations (though no formal amendment was ever made), and 1987 saw the first election for the presidency, and the first woman president. Thereafter elections followed frequently. The first thirty years of the Society's existence had seen just three presidents; the next ten saw four come and three go. When, in 1998, the Society was revived after a period of suspension and the *Rules* came up for review, the departure from the constitution was discovered. The importance of a permanent link with the Department was paramount; but it seemed retrograde to abandon a democratic tradition of election in favour of an *ex officio* coronation. A typically British compromise was agreed: the presidency would continue to be an elected office, but candidates would be restricted to academic staff of the Department.

The future of the Society

The records relate a story that will be familiar to anyone involved in a voluntary society of this sort over the same period: a triumphant entry into the world followed by cycles of decline and resurgence. The nature of the records that survive inevitably paint a gloomy picture. It is, after all, the common task of treasurers to appeal for more subscribing members and to evoke the most golden of past ages in order to shame the leaden performance of the present. It is the common task of presidents to urge improved attendances worthy of the dignitaries who visit them. And it is the common task of secretaries to take such exhortations at face-value and to record them faithfully. None of this means necessarily that a society is failing in its mission, or is failing to meet the needs of the community at that particular time. In fact such exhortations can be regarded as testimony to the optimism of the organizers, who believe that things can and should be better than they are.

But societies do decline and die, as the Hull and District itself nearly did on its fortieth birthday, and there are good reasons for this. Voluntary societies and organizations have generally suffered badly since the 1960s, because of the increasing pressures of work for those who have it, because of the decline of the extended family and reduced access of those with young children to family members able to step in to baby-sit, and perhaps above all because of domestic central heating and the television. The choice between going out into the cold and wet for intellectual stimulation and putting one's feet up at home is not a terribly difficult one. The choice may, however, be between one meeting and another, and in a city like Hull – an urban island set in a largely rural sea – cultural events often compete with one another for a limited clientele.

A theological society, however, provides both theology and society. It is an opportunity to discuss what has just been heard with like- and unlike-minded individuals, or simply the opportunity to gossip. Vital to the revival of the HDTS in 1998 was the recognition of this fact. Refreshments were now provided routinely, and meetings were moved from raked lecture theatres to the more intimate setting of a seminar room. A perhaps extreme example of this social emphasis is provided by the Leicester branch of the William Temple Association, which has become a dining club where no lectures are given.

The reason why a theological society might die is in some cases the same as the reason for its inception. To take an obvious example: the generation that in its youth or early adulthood was inspired by the great moments in ecumenism – the founding of the World Council of Churches, the formation of the Church of South India, the new openness to other Christians apparent at Vatican II – has grown older and less able to attend meetings. The ecumenical project has itself faltered, and no subsequent generations have been inspired by it in the same way.

The key to survival is the ability of such societies continually to re-invent themselves, to adapt to the constantly changing ways in which issues of religion and spirituality impact upon people's lives. For a generation which can access expert opinion instantly through a myriad of documentary channels on TV, or by a careful search of the world-wide web, the attraction of a distinguished speaker coming to a provincial town may not be as great as once it was. But, as in 1956, there is still 'a large body of people searching for a view of the world and a way of life who realize that they cannot go far without facing religious questions'. The need to discuss these questions, to test one's own understanding and to learn from others, will remain, and the theological society – perhaps in a very different form – will continue to have a role.

Footnotes

1 On the nature and extent of the early buildings, see T. W. Bamford, *The University of Hull: The First Fifty Years* (Oxford: University Press, for the University of Hull, 1978), pp.214-47. Bamford addressed the Society, in 1974, on the subject of Thomas Arnold.
2 T. E. Jessop, *An Introduction to Christian Doctrine* (London: Nelson, 1960), p.v.
3 The motto of University College, Hull adopted in 1928, was 'Lampada Ferens' ('bearing the torch'), which neatly incorporated the name of its founder, Thomas Robinson Ferens. The form originally proposed by T. E. Jessop was 'In obscuritatem lampada ferens' ('bringing light into darkness'); but this was rejected in case it was misconstrued 'as a slight on the locality'. (See Bamford, *The University*, p.47.)
4 Bamford, *The University*, p.268.
5 Bamford, *The University*, p.147.
6 Jessop's major publications in this field include *Law and Love: A Study of the Christian Ethic* (London: Epworth Press, 1940), *Social Ethics: A Problem for the Teaching Church* (London: Epworth Press, 1952); *The Christian Morality* (London: Epworth Press, 1960); and *An introduction to Christian Doctrine* (London: Nelson, 1960).
7 For example, the History Department has close connections with the Hull branch of the Historical Association and the East Riding Archaeological Society. The Hull branch of the Classical Association continues to thrive in spite of the closure of the Classics Department in the early 1990s.
8 At Bournemouth, Hexham/Tynedale, Leicester and York. The Leicester branch is now a dining-only society.

On the Record
by Barbara M. Robinson BTh, MA

THE FIRST DECADE

In 1957, three years after the University of Hull had received its charter and become an independent seat of learning, Hull and District Theological Society came into being. Its foundation enhanced the long-standing tradition established by the University College of providing adult education at the highest level, and of promoting links between the University and the City.

The inaugural meeting took place in the University's Senior Common Room on the evening of 16 November 1956. It was convened by the Revd. E. J. Tinsley, Lecturer in Charge of the Department of Theology, who was joined by 21 men and women 'representative of clerical and lay interests in the district'. What prompted this initiative was the success of one-day schools arranged by Hull Council of Churches and the University's Adult Education Department, added to the growing number of extra-mural classes in theology and 'the general concern among both ministers and lay-folk for a revival of theological interest'.

Mr Tinsley said that he had received 45 written and several verbal indications of interest in a theological society, 'and this, together with the interest of those present, suggested that there was strong support for such a venture'. The discussion which followed was wholly in favour of forming a society. A title was chosen, and it was decided that meetings should be held monthly, except in the summer, and should take place mainly in Hull, but occasionally in outlying parts of the district. 'A day in mid-week and a time in the late afternoon or early evening were preferable.' Speakers of outstanding theological reputation covering a wide field of interest were to be sought, but members of the Society were also to be invited to take part. It was agreed to seek the patronage of the Archbishop of York, and if possible to commence the Society's programme with the Primate as speaker, 'some time near Easter 1957'. The creators of the new Society were therefore aiming high, and their confidence was to prove well-founded.

Pro-tem officers were elected, with the Revd. E. J. Tinsley as President, the Revd. J. E. Young as Secretary, and Mr I. R. Billingham as Treasurer. The committee comprised the Revd. J. Atkinson, the Revd. P. J. Thompson, the Revd. F. Baker and Mrs K. A. MacMahon, who were given power to co-opt. A yearly subscription of a modest 7s.6d was approved, and the preparation of a syllabus of meetings and a simple constitution were left to the committee to work out in detail.

At a meeting held immediately afterwards, it was decided to invite Mr C. D. Bridge of Hull, Canon N. A. Vesey, of Beverley, and the Revd. Trevor T.

Rowe of Sutton to serve on the committee. It was also at this meeting that the decision was taken to make 'tentative inquiries' as to the possible association of members of the Jewish and Roman Catholic communities with the work of the Society.

Offers of contributions had already been received from three distinguished speakers – Prof. R L. Brett, on *Parallel Developments in the Fields of English and Biblical Criticism,* Prof. A. G. Dickens on *The Beginnings of Protestantism in Yorkshire,* and Dr Frank Baker on *The Methodist Love Feast.* One might say that the Hull and District Theological Society was off to a flying start.

* * * *

At the next meeting, on 29 November, Mr Thompson presided in the absence of Mr Tinsley. The annual subscription of 7s.6d was confirmed, and it was proposed that a charge of 2s.6d per member should be made for the opening part-session, though this idea was later dropped. Perhaps it was considered that the opening lectures should be a kind of gratuitous aperitif to whet the appetites of the audiences and encourage them to become paying members. Student subscriptions were set at 2s.6d.

It was decided to co-opt Fr. Patrick Cassidy to the committee to represent Roman Catholic interests, 'providing he felt free to serve in this way', and he was also listed among possible speakers. Fr. Cassidy, known, not surprisingly, as 'Butch' to his students at the Marist College in Hull, was a distinguished Cambridge scholar, but, as there is no further reference to him in the minutes, it would appear that he did not 'feel free'. It is believed that he moved to another appointment shortly afterwards, something which was common practice with the Marist Fathers.

In fact, the founders of the Society evidently did not find it easy to prevent it from becoming an exclusive club for Anglican clergy, for on 8 June 1962 it was recorded that, despite the rule that not all members should be ministers of religion and that the committee should include at least one Roman Catholic, one Jew and two members of different Protestant bodies, seven of the nine committee members were ministers and six of these were Anglicans!

A programme drafted by the president for the period May 1957 to June 1958 was given general approval, and further names of possible speakers were added by the members of the committee.

It was intended that the meeting in May 1958 should be held in Beverley if possible, but according to the printed programme it took place at the Hull Municipal Training College, with the assistance of the Principal, Dr Helena Todd. Mr E. J. Sewell, who delivered a paper on *Authority,* was substituting for the advertised speaker, the Lord Bishop of Bradford.

With bookings having to be made so far in advance, and taking into account the demanding lives of the distinguished clerics and academics involved, it is hardly surprising that changes had to be made, sometimes at short notice, but it is amazing how smoothly most of the sessions appeared to run, and the Society always seemed to be able to present an excellent speaker, even if he or she was not the one orginally advertised.

The Rules
A draft Constitution prepared by the Revd. P. J. Thompson was worked through in detail at the meeting on 29 November, and finally approved by the committee, but 'it was felt that a short Constitution and by-laws might prove to be more workable'.

The file copy of the Society's original rules is, however, quite detailed and precise:

It stipulates that the purpose of the organisation shall be 'the promotion of the study of theology in all its branches, as commonly recognised in the universities of Great Britain, within the University of Hull, the City of Kingston upon Hull, and the parts of Yorkshire and Lincolnshire round about'.

Membership was open to anyone over the age of 16, 'residing in these parts'. It may seem odd that a learned society devoted to serious discussion would pitch the age so low. They were obviously hoping to attract 6th-formers. We tend now to distinguish rather sharply between the capabilities of 16- and 18-year-olds, but at a time when the age of majority was still 21 (and remained so until 1970) and when universities still served, at least nominally, as the guardian of an undergraduate's morals *in loco parentis*, the difference was perhaps not perceived to be so great.

Application was to be made in writing to the Secretary, who would bring the name before the committee at its next ordinary meeting and inform the applicant if he or she had been elected. The Society reserved the right to terminate any member's connection with it by a resolution at the Annual General Meeting 'of which a week's written notice must be given'.

A member might introduce a guest without charge at any ordinary meeting, but could not bring the same guest more than once in one calendar year. The number of honorary members was limited to 20.

It is a reminder of the postwar times that, in addition to students in residence at a recognised school, college or university, 'persons doing National Service' could avail themselves of the reduced subscription of 2s.6d. together with others 'at the discretion of the committee'. Subscriptions became due annually on 1 September.

The officers of the Society were to be the Patron, the President, the Secretary and the Treasurer. The Patron would be the Archbishop of York 'for the time being', and the President the Lecturer or other University officer for the time being in charge of the Department of Theology. The Secretary and the Treasurer would be chosen from among the members of the Society and elected at an Annual General Meeting. They would serve for three years, after which they would be eligible for re-election.

The business of the Society was to be carried on by a committee consisting of the President, who would normally take the chair, the Secretary, the Treasurer and six members elected annually at the Annual General Meeting. 'Of these six, one shall always be a member of the teaching staff of the University of Hull, and one a member of the Department of Adult Education in the University.' The committee had power to co-opt up to four more members, and the quorum was set at five.

The Annual General Meeting was to be held in June each year 'if possible', and always within 15 months of the last such meeting. Ordinary meetings would take place in the course of each calendar year, except in July and August. 'These will normally be devoted to the reading and discussion of papers of theological interest. The committee shall try to see that a balance is struck between theorists and practitioners, amateurs and professionals, residents and non-residents in the choice of readers, and between the branches of, and relation to, theology in the choice of papers.'

A fee, on top of out-of-pocket expenses, might be paid to visiting speakers at the discretion of the committee. The normal place of meeting would be the University, but one meeting each year would be outside the City of Hull. Times of meetings would be varied to suit different groups of members, and no meeting was to last more than two hours.

Readers were to be asked to supply the Secretary with the text of their papers 'or an abstract thereof', and at least one meeting every year was to be given to the discussion of a number of short papers contributed by members.

Preparations

So, by the end of November 1956, plans for the first season of the new Society, May 1957 to June 1958, had been completed and a set of Rules drawn up. But more preparation needed to be done:

The first committee meeting of 1957 took place in the University's Senior Common Room at 4.30pm on 14 March, when it was agreed that the 2s.6d. levy suggested for the meetings before September should not be made, and that Jewish and Roman Catholic representation should be left with the President.

Before he had a chance to make his mark as founder-secretary, the Revd. J. E. Young announced that he was leaving the district, and his place was taken by the Revd. Trevor T. Rowe. Already, applications for membership had been received from 16 clergy and ministers, 25 lay people and five students. All of these were approved except two, 'concerning whom the Secretary was asked to seek further information'.

In view of the rule that 'any person over the age of 16 residing in these parts' would be eligible, one wonders what the grounds for refusal might be. It seems hardly likely that anyone under 16 would apply, so perhaps it had something to do with the residential requirement. It is also recorded that on 29 April 1957, 34 out of 35 applications were approved, but there is no clue as to why the other one was rejected.

Clearly, the committee were anxious to persuade people to join: 'Various suggestions were made of ways by which more people could be made aware of the formation of the Society.' Printed membership cards with the detailed programme were being made ready for the May meeting.

First event
The minutes record that the speaker at that first meeting on 9 May was to be Dr. F. W. Dillistone, but no further details are given, and the May and June meetings are not listed on the printed card.

One might have expected that the Society would be launched with a flourish, but perhaps the first event, notwithstanding the high reputation of the speaker, was regarded as a sort of experimental curtain-raiser to the main series of lectures starting in September, setting a standard but keeping a low profile. How would it go? How many would come? There may be a clue in the starting time of the meeting – 7.45pm, 15 minutes later than the others in the series, suggesting that Dr Dillistone may have had to come a long way. Maybe he did not announce his subject until he arrived, though that seems unlikely, and one is left wondering at this gap in the otherwise meticulous records.

* * * *

In addition to approving all but one of 35 applications for membership, the committee decided on 29 April that the President and Secretary should have power to invite to the meeting on 14 June (the first AGM) 'any ministers leaving the district in September who would like to attend, and also to invite as guests for one meeting any clergy or ministers moving into the district'.

It was agreed to purchase a guest book – intended, no doubt, to carry many distinguished signatures in the succeeding years. If such a book were ever purchased, it has unfortunately not survived.

Although the inaugural meeting had taken place only seven months previously, the first Annual General Meeting was duly held on Friday, 14 June, 1957, at 5pm, in accordance with the Rules. The 'A3' in the heading of the minutes presumably indicates that the venue was one of the University's lecture theatres.

Before that, at 4pm, the committee had met in the Senior Common Room, where they approved a further 20 applications for membership, and agreed to recommend to the AGM that at this stage only two honorary members should be elected to the Society, the Archbishop of York, according to the Rules and for his contribution to theology, and Prof. G. E. T. Mayfield,

Head of the Adult Education Department, for his services in the promotion of the study of theology in the district.

This recommendation was accepted by the full assembly, consisting of the President and 26 members, who also approved the Rules and confirmed the election of officers and committee members. Mr J. T. Ellis and Mr L. Fenney were appointed as auditors. It was announced that the Society now had a membership of 110, made up of 38 clergy and ministers, 66 lay people and six students. Dr Atkinson outlined a plan for beginning a Theological Seminar in association with the Department of Adult Education – evidence that the Society was already aiming to expand, even before launching its first lecture season. It would seem, too, that in appealing to members to offer to read papers to the Society, the President was actually preaching to the converted, for three of them had already volunteered to do so.

After the business meeting, papers were presented by Mr I. R. Billingham, on *Recent studies in St Matthew,* the Revd. T. T. Rowe, on *The Study of St Augustine,* and the Revd. L. C. Stanbridge, Rector of Cottingham and later Archdeacon of York, on *Richard Baxter – a 17th-Century Ecumenist.*

Patronal visit

On 11 October, 1957, plans were made to entertain the Society's patron, the Archbishop of York, Dr Michael Ramsey, who was to give an address the following month. Perhaps, after the somewhat low-key early events, this was to be regarded as the true launch celebration. It was agreed to hold a dinner in the Employees' Refectory, at which the guests would include Professors Mayfield, Dickens, Brett and Jessop, and Mr Richardson. With an eye to economy, the officers and committee would be invited to attend 'and pay their expenses'.

Despite the evident upsurge of interest in theology among the intelligentsia of Hull, shown by the growing number of members, the Society as yet had no reserves of cash, so the expenses of the guests were to be met 'by an arrangement fixed by the officers between the Department of Theology and the Society when the exact costs were known' – a delicate handling of an impecunious situation!

* * * *

The first committee meeting of 1958 was held on 14 February. There were only four people present, the President, in the chair, the Revds. P. J. Thompson and T. T. Rowe and Mr I. R. Billingham, but this was probably due to the fact that a meeting of the Society was taking place on the same night, no doubt to guarantee attendance. In any event, the quartet got through quite a lot of business including the forward planning of speakers, reaching as far as the spring of 1960, when Dr Austin Farrar was to be asked to give a paper in April or May.

A number of applications for membership were received and approved, and a letter was read from the *Hull Daily Mail,* noting that the meetings of the Society were private but expressing a willingness to receive copy after the events. Requests to the News Editor for coverage of social events always exceeded the number of reporters available, especially in the evenings, and, naturally, 'hard news' had to take priority, so arrangements of this kind were often made. This provided useful publicity for the organisation concerned, and also enabled the newspaper to carry prestigious items written by experts who were familiar with any esoteric language involved – though if space was short the next day much of the carefully-prepared script might end up on the 'spike'.

Then, as now, societies with somewhat similar agendas and specialised appeal found the need to avoid meeting on the same day, and it was suggested that the Secretary should consult his opposite number at the Historical Association to try to prevent the clashing of dates. It takes a lot of seven-and-sixpences to make a comfortable balance-in-hand, but although the Treasurer was able to announce a sum of only £17, it was decided to spend a little of it on some headed notepaper for the use of the officers. Keeping up appearances was clearly a priority.

* * * *

Opening the meeting on 16 May 1958, President Tinsley told the committee that he had sent a message of sympathy on behalf of the Society to Mrs Manson, on hearing of the death of Prof. William Manson, who was to have given a paper, *Moses in the New Testament,* at the Annual General Meeting.

Two applications for membership were received and approved, and the Secretary reported that the Society now had 153 members of whom 42 (27.4%) were ministers and 19 (12.4%) were members of the University staff. (The figures given at the subsequent AGM added 72.6% lay people.)

The Treasurer's report, however, was less encouraging: the balance-in-hand had fallen to £14 and 33 subscriptions had not been received, of which 10 were owed by students. Some things never change. Understandably – and perhaps unconsciously aptly worded – 'the matter of a Society dinner was left on the table'.

The 1958-59 programme was now virtually complete, and the Secretary was authorised to explore the possibility of a joint meeting with the Historical Association. All this was reported to the Annual General Meeting on 12 June 1958, when the committee were re-elected and the Treasurer's report approved. There had been a total income for the year of £41.10s.and the final balance-in-hand was £15 1s 1d.

A paper was read by Dr Richard Hanson in place of that which was to have been delivered by Prof. Manson.

PROGRAMME 1957-1958

Friday, 27 September 1957
 Prof A. G. Dickens, *The Origins of Protestantism in Yorkshire*.
Friday, 11 October
 The Presidential Address, *Liturgical Mysticism in the Bible*.
Friday, 8 November
 The Lord Archbishop of York, *The Concept of Sacrifice in Christian Theology*.
Friday 6 December
 The Revd. Dr. J Atkinson, *Luther and St. John*.
Thursday, 16 January 1958
 The Revd. Prof. H. H. Rowley, *The Dead Sea Scrolls*.
Friday, 14 February
 The Revd. P. J. Thompson, *St John's First Epistle and Psalm 119*.
Friday, 14 March
 Prof. R. L. Brett, *Parallels in Contemporary Biblical and Literary Criticism*.
Friday, 11 April
 The Revd. Chancellor R. L. Cant, *The Anglican Theology of John Henry Newman*.
Monday, 5 May
 Mr E. J. Sewell, *Authority*. (Meeting held at the Hull Municipal Training College.)
Thursday, 12 June
 Annual General Meeting, followed by a paper given by Dr Richard Hanson, Senior Lecturer in Theology at Nottingham University, *Allegory and Typology in Interpreting Scripture*.

Reaching out

The final committee meeting of 1958 took place on 3 October, when a more cheerful Treasurer was able to report that a good number of people had renewed their membership.

Because Dr Norman Sykes was to give a lecture in the University on 19 November, it was agreed to cancel the meeting of the Society planned for that date and to ask Dr Baker to give his paper at a joint meeting of the Society and the Historical Association on 13 April 1959.

Reaching out into the City, programmes had been distributed to the Public Library the Vice-Chancellor, the Honorary Members, the Senior Common Room and the Historical Association. The Secretary was asked to send cards to the Bishop of Hull and the Swedish Pastor. A membership list was to be drawn up and circulated in November.

The committee also decided to invite the Revd. L. C. Stanbridge and Mr E. J.Sewell to become co-opted members of the committee.

The following – all eminent theological scholars and authors – were to be invited to give papers in the 1959-1960 session, and the suggested fees are rather significant, in view of subsequent inflation:

> Mark Tweedy C.R. (3 guineas)
> Gervasse Mathew O.P. (5 guineas)
> Dr Gordon Rupp (5 guineas)
> Mr G. W. Anderson (3 guineas)
> Mr Leeny (3 guineas) (no doubt the Revd. A. R. C. Leaney)

By April 1959, plans were well advanced for the third season: The Revd. Mark Tweedy had agreed to come on 30 October to give a paper entitled *A Monk's Visit to Russia,* which was to feature a film. The Revd. Gervasse Mathew was also booked for 28 April 1960 to give an illustrated talk on *Recent Discoveries in Byzantine Art,* Prof. E. G. Rupp had promised a paper on Thomas Munzer, Hans Huth and *The Gospel of All Creation* in November or December, and 7 November was chosen.

A list was drawn up from which the Secretary was to obtain three further speakers, those to be approached first being Prof. Nineham, Mr W. A. Whitehouse and Prof. H. H. Farmer. Papers were to be invited from three local people, the Revd. W. Richardson, Miss R. Woolf and the Revd. P. Thieme, and short papers from the Revd. G. Christie, Mr H. W. Blanchard and Mr Batchelor.

It was agreed that Prof. S. H. Hooke, who was to speak on the Dead Sea Scrolls the following month, should be accommodated at the Royal Station Hotel and that the Society should be responsible for the bill, together with first-class travelling expenses and a fee of five guineas. The Chairman suggested that the Department of Theology would be willing to entertain the Professor and the members of the committee to dinner.

Still on the subject of refreshments, the meeting also decided that coffee should be served at the close of Dr Easton's lecture on 27 April, 'and that the cost be borne by the Society'. Four applications for membership were approved, including one from the Bishop of Hull, and it was reported that membership was now just under 100, a considerable dip since the Annual Meeting. Time would show whether this was a trend, or just part of a fluctuating pattern.

* * * *

At the Annual General Meeting on 16 June 1959, the Secretary reported a total 'book' membership of 159, and said that for this year there were 88 paid-up members and 19 student members. All members were to be asked to renew their subscriptions for the year when the programmes for that session were ready.

Committee members elected to serve for the year 1959-1960 were: the Revds. P. J. Thompson, J. Atkinson, F. Baker, G. Christie, and L. C. Stanbridge and Mr E. J. Sewell. The Secretary was asked to write letters of thanks to

Mrs MacMahon and Mr Bridge, who had indicated their desire to stand down. On the committee's nomination, it was agreed to invite Prof. T. E. Jessop, Ferens Professor of Philosophy at Hull University, to accept Honorary Membership of the Society. The meeting decided to change the word 'will' to 'may' in the rule stating that 'one meeting each year will be outside the City of Hull'. Perhaps it was proving difficult to find suitable locations further afield. At the close of business, papers were read by members of the Society.

There are some items of expenditure on Treasurer Billingham's balance sheet for the year, which are perhaps worth noting: Hull Corporation had made a charge of 6s for the use of the Training College for Mr Sewell's paper; Dr Ward's visit had cost 10s, Canon Greenslade's £6.7s.6d, and Prof. Barrett's £5.7s.6d, while Prof. Hooke's lecture had set the Society back £15.4s. The coffee had cost £2.4s.1d. The balance in hand, however, was still a healthy £15.17s.11d.

PROGRAMME 1958-1959

Friday, 24 October, 1958
    The Rt. Revd. Dr. J. W. C. Wand, formerly Lord Bishop of London, *The Christian Interpretation of Christ in the light of modern thought*. (Open meeting in conjunction with the Department of Adult Education).

Wednesday, 19 November
    The Revd. Dr. F. Baker, *The Rise and Development of Methodism in the East Riding* (Meeting postponed until 13 April 1959).

Tuesday, 9 December
    The Revd R L. Cole, *Natural Theology: is it a legitimate inquiry?*

Friday, 16 January, 1959
    The Revd. Canon S. L. Greenslade, Ely Professor of Divinity, Cambridge University, *Episcopacy and Pastoral Care in the Early Church*.

Thursday, 26 February
    Mr C. B. Cox, Lecturer in English, Hull University, *The Literary Criticism of the Gospels*.

Friday, 13 March
    The Revd. Dr. C. K Barrett, Senior Lecturer in Theology, Durham University.

Monday, 27 April
    Dr. M. F. Easton, Staff Tutor in Art in the Department of Adult Education, Hull University, *Rembrandt as a Religious Artist* (illustrated).

Thursday, 21 May
    Prof. S. H. Hooke, *Symbolism in the Dead Sea Scrolls*.

Tuesday, 16 June
    AGM followed by short papers from the Revd. D. W. Foster, the Revd. R. E. Nixon and Pastor C.O.H. Werner, of the Hull German Lutheran

Church.

An Open Lecture was given in the Assembly Hall of the University on 15 October 1958 by the Very Revd. Dr. Norman Sykes on *The Elizabethan Settlement*.

Numbers steady

Plans for the year 1960-1961 were laid at a meeting on 15 December 1959. It was agreed to invite Mr W. A. Whitehouse, Prof. N. W. Porteous, Mr A. Robertson and Mr J. N. Sanders to visit the Society or, 'failing them', Mr A. G. B. Higgins, Dr J.G. Davies, Prof. A. Guilding and Prof. F. F. Bruce. Local speakers listed were Prof. Jessop, the Revd D. Carter and Dr. D. G. Charlton, or, 'failing them', Prof. Reece, Prof. Castle and Dr Douie. (It is perhaps indicative of the ambitions of the young society that Decima L. Douie, one of the most distinguished of Hull University's many distinguished medievalists, was considered only as the last of the third choices!)

Membership numbers were 'about the same as last year', and 14 applications were accepted. The Treasurer, who announced that he had about £20 in hand, added that so far 67 full and 11 student subscriptions had been paid.

* * * *

The fourth season was due to open with a musical flourish – a talk by Alec Robertson, *Johann Sebastian Bach, a Fifth Evangelist* – on 14 October 1960, and it was agreed by the committee at their meeting on 19 May that the Music Society and the Newman Circle should be informed about the event. The Treasurer stated that he expected that the expenditure for the year would be 'about the same as the income', and, when all was safely gathered in, the Society ended the session with a balance-in-hand of £19.11s.8d.

* * * *

By 16 June, the date of the AGM, speakers had been booked for all the meetings. The Secretary reported a 'book' membership of 156, with 73 paid-up members and 11 student members.

The meeting heard with regret that both the Secretary the Revd. Trevor T. Rowe, and the Treasurer, Mr I. R. Billingham, were leaving the district. President Tinsley thanked them for their services and presented them with small gifts on behalf of the Society They were replaced by Mr R. A. Whittle, as Secretary, and Mr E. J. Sewell, as Treasurer, joining a committee comprised of the Revd. P. J. Thompson, the Revd. Dr. J. Atkinson, the Revd. L. C. Stanbridge, Mr C. B. Freeman, the Revd. J. M. B. Dean and Brig. A. Goldsmith. The Secretary was asked to write a letter of thanks and good wishes to Prof. G. E. T. Mayfield, one of the Society's two Honorary Members, on his retirement. Business concluded, three papers were read by members of the Society, the Revd. G. Christie, Mr B. W. Blanchard and Mr C. B. Freeman

PROGRAMME 1959-1960

Friday, 30 October, 1959
> The Revd Mark Tweedy C. R., *A Monk's Visit to Russia,* illustrated by a film.

Wednesday, 18 November
> The Revd. Prof J. K. S. Reid, *Life in Christ.*

Wednesday, 16 December
> The Revd. P. Thieme, *The Old Catholic Church of Holland – its history and doctrine.*

Tuesday, 19 January
> The Revd . W. Richardson, *The Philosophical Defence of Christianity, today and in the Second Century.*

Monday, 15 February
> Miss R. Woolf, *Popular Meditation in the Middle Ages.*

March
> Meeting to be arranged (A scribbled pencil note suggests that the Revd. Barclay gave a talk entitled *God and no-gods,* but no date is given.)

Thursday, 28 April
> The Revd. Gervasse Mathew, *Recent discoveries in Byzantine Art* (illustrated). A joint meeting with the Newman Society.

Friday, 27 May
> The Revd. Prof C. E. Evans (Subject to be announced).

Thursday, 16 June
> AGM, followed by short papers from the Revd. G. Christie, *Scholarship and Devotion,* Mr B. W. Blanchard, *The Buildings of Nonconformity,* and Mr C. B. Freeman, *The Golden Age of the English Hymn.*

Looking Ahead

At a meeting on 20 October 1960, it was reported that 50 members had renewed their subscriptions so far. Programmes had been distributed and the Secretary was asked to send cards to the Municipal Training College and the library of the Institute of Education.

Looking ahead to l961-1962, it was decided to invite some 14 speakers to visit the Society: Miss A. Guilding, A. C. Bouquet, J. Heywood Thomas, Prof. W. R. Niblett, the Revd. Raymond George (or Dr Alan Kay), J. F. Torrance, Prof. J. G. Davies, Prof. Castle, Prof. Rees, Pastor I .Bergmark, Pastor C. O. H. Werner, the Revd. K. Tucker and the Revd. S. Walker.

The final committee meeting of 1960 took place on 9 December, and finance was a major consideration. It was reported that 63 members had paid their subscriptions to date. A list of those who had belonged during the previous two years had been duplicated and circulated to all members, and it was suggested that those who had not yet renewed their subscriptions should be asked to do so as soon as possible. The balance-in-hand was approximately £9.10s. There were fees and expenses for three visiting speakers to be met, and it was hoped that further subscriptions would be forthcoming to help meet these and avoid a deficit. It was decided that, in future, visiting speakers should be offered second-class rail fares and a fee of 2 guineas or 4 guineas, 'according to their standing', this latter to be decided by the committee – an unenviable task, no doubt something like the Judgment of Paris with brains, not beauty, as the deciding factor!

The Secretary reported that speakers had been booked for October and November 1961 and February, May and June 1962. Prof. Aileen Guilding had also promised to come if a suitable date could be arranged.

Several more prospective speakers were suggested, including the Hull Communal Rabbi, Dr. Chaim J. Cooper, and it was proposed that the Institute of Education should be approached with a view to making Prof. Niblett's visit in November a joint one, as his subject, *Essentials in Religious Education,* should be of interest to many teachers who were not members of the Society.

'Precarious'

Hardly had Mr Sewell taken office as Treasurer when he received an appointment as Lecturer in Divinity at Bede College Durham, and was to take up his duties there on 1 April 1961. This was good news for Mr Sewell but a loss to the Society, which speeded him on his way with thanks and good wishes at a committee meeting on 10 February 1961. The Revd. K. R. Tucker was invited to serve as Acting Treasurer until the AGM.

Paid-up membership at that stage was 66, made up of 57 members paying 7s.6d and nine students at 2s.6d. The committee, meeting on 31 May, did not consider this to be satisfactory – the total should be nearer 100 – and the question of publicity was discussed. The Acting Treasurer, Mr Tucker, described the financial position as 'rather precarious', as the balance was almost non--existent. Heavy expenditure had been incurred for printed stationery and expenses for visiting speakers. 'The former was non-recurring and the latter was being kept to a minimum for the forthcoming session.'

Further blows to the Society were announced at the same time: Mr Whitta, appointed Secretary at the previous AGM, was leaving the district, and Brig. Goldsmith was also on the move. It was agreed to nominate Miss M. Fussell as Secretary and Miss Stonehouse or Mrs Shorter for appointment to the committee.

The President told the meeting that he had written to the retiring

Archbishop of York, Dr. Michael Ramsey thanking him for serving the Society as Patron, and that he had offered to write to Dr.Ramsey's successor, Dr Donald Coggan, inviting him to be the new Patron.

* * * *

At the Annual General Meeting on 2 June 1961, the 'book' membership stood at 'approximately 100', but the accounts told a different story: Subscriptions added up to only £22.10s. and after all expenses had been met there was only £2.14s.9d. in the bank and £1 in hand.

But, undaunted, the show went on. An outline of the programme for 1961-1962 was presented, indicating that speakers had been booked for all the meetings.

The committee now comprised: The Revds. P. J. Thompson, Dr. J. Atkinson, L. C. Stanbridge, J. M. B. Dean and D. Carter, and Mr C. B. Freeman. Mrs J. Shorter was co-opted. The search was still on for representatives of the Roman Catholic, Jewish and Nonconformist communities – though, of course, Rabbi Cooper had agreed to give a lecture in 1961.

At the close of business, papers were read by the Revd. Canon S. Stevenson, and the Revd. G. A. Bannister.

PROGRAMME 1960-1961

Friday, 14 October, 1960
   Mr Alec Robertson, *Johann Sebastian Bach, a Fifth Evangelist.*
Monday, 7 November
   The Revd. Prof. E. Gordon Rupp. Professor of Ecclesiastical History, Manchester University, *Thomas Muntzer, Hans Huth and 'The Gospel of All Creatures'.*
Friday, 9 December
   The Revd. D. Carter, Vicar of St Alban, Hull, *Luther as Exegete.*
Thursday, 12 January, 1961
   Prof. T. E. Jessop, Ferens Professor of Philosophy, Hull University, *Some Problems of Christian Ethics.*
Friday, 17 February
   The Revd. W. A. Whitehouse, Principal, St Cuthbert's Society and Reader in Divinity, Durham University, *There is no Authority except from God.*
Tuesday, 21 March
   The Revd. J. N. Sanders, Fellow of Peterhouse and Lecturer in Divinity, Cambridge University, *St. John on Patmos.*
Tuesday, 11 April
   The Revd. Dr. Ulrich E. Simon, Reader in Theology, King's College, London University, *Mysticism in the Old Testament.*

Wednesday, 10 May
> Dr. D.G. Charlton, Senior Lecturer in French, Hull University, *Some Nineteenth-Century Substitutes for Christianity*.

Friday, 2 June
> AGM. The Revd. Canon S. Stevenson, Vicar of St Augustine, Hull, *St Thomas Aquinas' Conception of Grace*. The Revd. G. A. Bannister, Minister of Prospect Street Presbyterian Church, Hull, *Athanasius Contra Aquinas*.

New President

From 1962, the Society's minute-book contains only the records of Annual General Meetings, which makes things easier for the chronicler but reduces the amount of detail available.

By 8 June 1962, further changes were having to be made. The Founder President, the Revd. E. J. Tinsley, was leaving Hull for Leeds. The Revd. L. C. Stanbridge thanked him for the work he had done for the Society, 'both in founding it and throughout its existence', and wished him every happiness.

As no Professor of the Department had then been appointed, it was resolved that 'unless such an appointment was made before the next session, the Acting Head of the Department of Theology should be asked to be the Acting President of the Society'. However, before the next AGM, Mr Tinsley had been succeeded by the Revd. Prof. Anthony T. Hanson.

Concern was again expressed at falling membership. The 1961-1962 figures of 51 paid-up members and six students were compared unfavourably with the two previous sessions, and ways of increasing the numbers were discussed. It was resolved that: The printed programme card should no longer be used as a receipt for subscription, but should be used to advertise the events of the coming year. New appointments to the district should be contacted and representatives should be appointed from each denomination and profession to ensure that this happened. Schools should be circulated with the events of the coming year. Programme cards should be displayed on all church notice boards and on the main display board in the Hull Reference Library. The names of leading speakers should be sent to the *Hull Daily Mail* for publication.

The meeting also passed an amendment to the Constitution, now requiring that the officers of the committee should consist of: A President; two Vice-Presidents, to hold office for three years; Secretary and Treasurer; six committee members and four co-opted members 'if the committee so desired'.

Mrs J.B.Tanner*, a member of the University staff, had succeeded Miss

---

*This was the new Secretary's modest way of referring to herself. She was, in fact; Dr Mary Tanner, an Old Testament scholar and a distinguished ecumenical theologian, now a holder of the Order of the British Empire and European President of the World Council of Churches.

Fussell as Secretary, and it was agreed that she and the Treasurer, Mr Tucker, should both continue for a further year.

The Revd. L. C. Stanbridge and the Revd. J. Dean were resigning from the committee, and the four remaining members, the Revd. P. Thompson, Dr. J. Atkinson, the Revd. D. Carter and Mr C. B. Freeman were re-elected. They were to be joined by Pastor I. Bergmark, of the Swedish church, and the Revd. G. Burt. It was further agreed that the committee should be asked to co-opt Mrs Shorter for a second year, together with Dr. Proctor, Mr D. Dermott and one student.

Business concluded, papers were read by the Revd. S. Walker and the Revd. K. Tucker.

PROGRAMME 1961-1962

Wednesday, 18 October 1961
> The Revd. J. Heywood Thomas, Lecturer in Philosophy of Religion at Manchester University, *History and the Belief in the Resurrection.*

Wednesday, 8 November
> Prof. W. R. Niblett, Dean of the London Institute of Education, *Essentials in Religious Education.*

Thursday, 7 December
> Rabbi Dr. Chaim J. Cooper, Communal Rabbi of Hull, *The Jewish Doctrine of Man's Sin and Atonement.*

Friday, 19 January, 1962
> Mrs J. Tanner (Dr Mary Tanner), Assistant Lecturer in Theology at Hull University, *Some Recent Developments in Old Testament Studies.*

Thursday, 22 February
> The Revd. Prof. J.G. Davies, Edward Cadbury Professor of Theology at Birmingham University, *Baptismal Theology and Architecture.*

Monday, 19 March
> Pastor I. Bergmark, Swedish Pastor in Hull, *The Authority of the Bible.*

Friday, 27 April
> Prof. Aileen Guilding, Professor of Biblical History and Literature at Sheffield University, *'To the Hebrews', a sermon for Pentecost,*

Wednesday, 23 May
> The Revd. A. Raymond George, Principal of Wesley College, Headingley, *Anamnesis and Oblation.*

Friday, 8 June
> AGM. The Revd. S. Walker, Vicar of St. Mary, Beverley, *Faith and Reason.* The Revd. K. Tucker, Minister of Sutton Methodist Church, *Some Fourth-Century Problems of Church and State.*

In the red

Falling membership was again at the top of the agenda at the Annual General Meeting on 14 June 1963, by which time the numbers had dropped to 36 paid-up members and nine student members.

'Over four years the membership could be seen to be rapidly declining,' and the meeting went on to discuss ways of increasing the numbers. These included several of the ideas put forward at the previous AGM, and, in addition, a circular was to be sent out in September to Anglican clergy, Methodist, Baptist and Congregational ministers, local preachers and teachers.

The drop in subscriptions inevitably hit the Society in the pocket: 'Owing to the decline in membership and the expenses incurred by a series of lecturers from other parts of the country, the Society no longer had a reserve fund from which to begin the next session. It was hoped that expenses in the next session would be much lower, as only two of the speakers were from outside the City.'

The accounts for the year show that speakers' expenses had amounted to £23.14s.9d., printing £2.10s, coffee £3.16s.3d, Staff Refectory £2.1s.1d., postage £1.1s., and Treasurer's expenses 7s., a total of £33.10s.1d. This was offset by £15.15s in subscriptions, £1.10s 'coffee money', a donation of 3s.and 6s.10d Bank interest, amounting to only £17.14s.10d. This had eaten up the reserve of £15.13s.7d, leaving the Society 1s.8d in the red – a trifle, no doubt, but we all know Mr Micawber's views on insolvency.

After some discussion, it was decided to raise the subscription to 10s for full membership and 5s for student membership. 'These subscriptions would include coffee at each meeting and therefore save the Treasurer the inconvenience of collecting money.'

Turning to other matters, the meeting elected the Revd. P. J. Thompson and Mr C. B. Freeman as the first two Vice-Presidents of the Society. The Secretary, Mrs J.B. Tanner, and the Treasurer, the Revd. K.Tucker, agreed to continue in office, and Mr L. Fenney was elected auditor.

Dr. J. Atkinson, the Revd. D. Carter, the Revd. G. Burt and Mrs M. Shorter were re-elected and they were to be joined on the committee by the Revd.G. R. Bell. As before, they were empowered to co-opt others 'if a larger committee were felt to be necessary'.

There is, of course, an optimum size for a committee, depending on the nature of the organisation it serves: too small, and it tends to become a one-man (or woman) band, dominated by the strongest personality; too large and we know the saying about a camel being a horse designed by a committee.

The AGM ended with the reading of papers by the Revd. G. M. Burt and the Revd. J. V. Carroll SM, Headmaster of the Marist College.

PROGRAMME 1962-1963

Tuesday, 18 October, 1962
    Dr. N. Zernov, *The significance of the Russian Church.*
Friday, 9 November
    Prof. R. N. Smart, *Hindu Theology and its relation to Christianity.*

Tuesday, 11 December
   The Lord Archbishop of York, *The Revision of the Psalter.*
Tuesday, 22 January, 1963
   The Revd. Prof. A. S. Herbert, *The place of the Old Testament in the life of the Church.*
Friday, 15 February
   The Revd. P. Hammond, *Architecture and Ecclesiology.*
Tuesday, 7 March
   Miss M. Boaden, *Calvin's Doctrine of the Church.*
Thursday, 25 April
   The Revd. A. R. C. Leaney, *The Jesus of History.*
Thursday, 16 May
   The Revd. G. S. Wakefield, *Puritan Mysticism.*
Friday, 14 June
   AGM. The Revd. G. M. Burt, *John Wesley's Doctrine of Baptism in relation to the Eighteenth Century.* The Revd. J. V. Carroll, SM (Subject not given).

Rules reviewed

The Society's Founder President, the Revd. Prof. E. J. Tinsley, was honoured at the next Annual General Meeting by being made an Honorary Member.

Much of the business part of the meeting, which took place on 8 May 1964, was taken up by a review of the Rules, and a number of changes were made:

The new subscription rates were confirmed, together with the decision to appoint two Vice-Presidents.

The six committee members now had to include 'a student of the Department of Theology'.

The date of the AGM was moved from June to May.

Rule 8c, stating that 'The normal place of meeting shall be within the precincts of the University but one meeting each year will be outside the City of Hull', which had already been amended by changing the word 'will' to 'may', was now deleted altogether. Maybe the committee were finding it too difficult to secure affordable meeting-places outside the University.

The number of auditors to be appointed annually was reduced from two to one.

The Treasurer reported that for the current session there were 35 paid-up members and nine student members.

The two Vice-Presidents, the Revd. P. Thompson and Mr C. B. Freeman, were re-elected for a further year. Mrs Tanner agreed to continue as Secretary, Mr E. Baslington was elected Treasurer, and Mr Fenney continued as Auditor.

The 1964-1965 committee comprised the Revd. Dr. J. Atkinson, the Revd. D. Carter, the Revd. G. Burt and the Revd. G. Bell, who were all re-elected. Mrs M. Swinburne and Mr R. Gill were elected. It was agreed to co-opt a member of the Department of Adult Education.

The meeting ended with the reading of papers by the Revd. L. C. Stanbridge and Mr C. G. Bridge.

PROGRAMME 1963-1964

Thursday, 24 October, 1963
  The Revd. Prof. A. T. Hanson, *Typology*.
Friday, 15 November
  The Revd. Prof. E. J. Tinsley, *The Prophet, the Mystic and the Poet*.
Friday, 8 December
  The Revd. H. Moulton, *Bible Translating*.
Tuesday, 28 January, 1964
  Students of the Department of Theology, Hull University.
Thursday, 20 February
  Father A. Storey, *The relationship between the Last Supper and Calvary in the Roman Catholic Mass*.
Friday, 6 March
  Miss E. I. Pinthus, *The Biblical Basis of Quakerism*.
Tuesday, 28 April
  Dr. Peter Brooks, *Full Circle: a study in the development of Thomas Cranmer's understanding of the Eucharist*.
Friday, 8 May
  AGM. Short papers by the Revd. L. C. Stanbridge and Mr C. G. Bridge.

By 20 May 1965, the Treasurer was able to tell the Annual General Meeting that the Society was in a much better position than at the end of the previous season, 'having £7 in hand'. This was due, he was obliged to add, not to an increase in membership but to the low expenditure on 'outside' speakers, and he went on to warn the gathering that, unless membership increased, the position would be more serious at the end of the next session.

There was, however, evidence that the work accomplished over the previous eight years must have sparked fresh enthusiasm for the subject among the young: the minutes record that the Society sent its best wishes to a new student Theological Society – The 142 Society – so called because the theology lecturers used the house at 142 Cottingham Road as the departmental headquarters.

One may perhaps wonder why the students did not come forward to boost the falling membership of the established Society, but the generation gap is no new phenomenon. 'Crabbed age and youth cannot live together,' said Shakespeare, and the young have always felt uneasy in the company of those older – and arguably wiser – than themselves, preferring to socialise with their own contemporaries. The Society had probably done well to keep the half-dozen or so student members still on its books.

Prof. Hanson thanked Mrs Tanner for serving as Secretary for the previous four years She now moved over to the committee, replacing Mrs Swinburne, who resigned. The role of Secretary was taken by the Revd. Ian N. McPherson, and the remaining members of the committee were re-elected along with the two Vice-Presidents and the Treasurer. The meeting closed with papers read by Mr J. Biggs and the newly elected Secretary, Mr McPherson.

PROGRAMME 1964-1965

Friday, 23 October, 1964
   The Revd. G. S. M. Walker, Lecturer in Church History and Doctrine, Leeds University, *The Eucharistic Debate of the Ninth Century.*
Friday, 20 November
   The Revd Prof. R. P. C. Hanson, Professor of Theology, Nottingham University, *The Function and Status of the Bible.*
Thursday, 8 December
   Mr R. G. Swinburne, Lecturer in Philosophy, Hull University, *God Outside Time.*
Tuesday, 19 January, 1965
   Students of the Department of Theology, Hull University.
Wednesday, 10 February
   The Revd. Cornelius Ernst O. P., Hawkesyard Priory, Staffordshire, *The Theology of Grace.*
   Joint Newman Circle and Theological Society meeting.
Thursday, 4 March
   Dr. J. Meeres, Lecturer in Religion, Hull Municipal Training College, *Christian marriage as illustrating the relationship of Church and State in the Twentieth Century.*
Friday, 23 April
   Dr. K. W. Andrews, Industrial Scientist, Sheffield, *Science, Sense and Worship.*
Monday, 3 May
   The Revd. R. E. Davies, Lecturer at Didsbury College, Bristol, *Authority in Religion: the Problems Today.*
Thursday, 20 May
   AGM. Papers by Dr. J. Briggs, Lecturer in Chemistry, Hull University, and The Revd. I. N. McPherson, Minister of the Zion Congregational Church, Cottingham.

'Angels'

Clearly, what the Society needed were what the theatrical world calls 'angels' – supporters or sponsors willing to put their hands in their pockets. At the Annual General Meeting on 17 May 1966, Treasurer Baslington was able to report that the Society was in a sound financial position. This was due partly to a decrease in expenditure for coffee, and partly to a number of special donations which had been received. But then came the customary warning that, unless membership increased, the position would be more serious at the end of the next session, and he suggested that members of the committee should help him to collect subscriptions, particularly at the first meeting of the new season.

Ian McPherson resigned from the Secretaryship, receiving the thanks of the President for his efficiency over the previous year, and was succeeded by the Revd. I. Ellis, who was elected to serve for three years. The student representative, Mr R. Gill, also resigned and was replaced by Mr D. Walker. The other members of the committee were re-elected, along with the two Vice-Presidents the Treasurer and the Auditor, so there was a good blend of experience and fresh minds on the executive as the Society ended its first decade. Speakers had been booked for most of the 1966-1967 meetings, though some dates and titles had still to be decided. Business concluded, papers were read by Mr D. Dermott and the Revd. A. H. R. Quinn, both members of the Society.

PROGRAMME. 1965-1966

Friday, 15 October, 1965
 The Revd. Prof. C. K. Barrett, Professor of Divinity, Durham University, *Paul's Quotations*.

Monday, 15 November
 Mr C. J. F. Williams, Lecturer in Philosophy, Hull University, *The Incarnation: Nature and Person*.

Tuesday, 7 December
 Mr A. K. Sen, Department of Psychology, and Mr R. C. Tyagi, Department of Physics, Hull University, *Some Aspects of Hinduism*.

Tuesday, 25 January, 1966
 Students of the Department of Theology, Hull University.

Friday, 18 February
 The Revd Prof. G. W. H. Lampe, Professor of Theology, Cambridge University, *Church Membership and Excommunication*. Joint Newman Circle and Theological Society meeting.

Friday, 4 March
 Miss M. D. Hooker, King's College, London University, *The Son of Man: an unorthodox defence of an orthodox view*.

Thursday, 14 April
 The Revd. D. Carter, Vicar of St Alban, Hull, *Theology in Paint*.

Tuesday, 17 May
> AGM. Short papers by Mr D. Dermott, Department of Theology, Hull University, *The Churchmanship of Alexander Knox,* and the Revd. A. H. R. Quinn, Church of England Chaplain, Hull University, *A Place of Covenant.*

Stability

Shortage of money was still causing concern when members met for the Annual General Meeting on 16 May 1967. While a balance of £6.11s was brought forward, cash in hand for the present year amounted to only 7s.4d. Total income, including a donation of £4, was £21.15s.10d, and there had been heavy expenses relating to speakers and printing. As an experiment, it was decided to discontinue meeting in Room S16 and to try Lecture Theatre B in the new Arts Block. This would reduce the cost of meetings, but Treasurer Baslington insisted that 'only a consistent subscribing membership enabled the Society to achieve any financial stability'.

A measure of stability was, however, achieved by the re-election of the two Vice-Presidents, the Secretary, Treasurer and Auditor, but there were several changes in the committee: Sister Mary Richard was elected in place of Miss M. Kay to represent the Endsleigh community, and Dr. R. N. Whybray and Mr K. Holroyd replaced Mrs M. E. Tanner and Dr. J. Atkinson. Mr W. T. Hicks was elected student representative, replacing Mr D. Walker.

A further change was announced concerning the joint meeting with the Hull Newman Circle, due to take place on 7 June: Fr. Laurence Bright O.P. would speak in place of the Revd. Charles Davis.

Papers were read to the AGM audience by Pastor E. H. Schaar and the Revd. H. C. West.

PROGRAMME 1966-1967

Tuesday, 18 October, 1966
> Prof. G. P. Malalasekera, the High Commissioner for Ceylon, *The Basic Doctrines of Buddha.*

Friday, 18 November
> Miss P. M. Harry, Royal Holloway College, London University, *Some Aspects of Seventeenth-Century French Free Thought.*

Wednesday, 7 December
> The Revd. I. Ellis, Department of Theology, Hull University, *Edwin Sandys: an Elizabethan Archbishop of York.*

Tuesday, 24 January, 1967
> Two short papers by students of the Department of Theology, Hull University.

Friday, 10 February
> The Revd. A. Gelston, Grey College, Durham University, *A Sidelight on the Son of Man.*

Thursday, 4 May
> The Revd. Dr. T. H. L. Parker, Vicar of Oakington, Cambridge, *The Commentaries of Lancelot Ridley.*

Tuesday, 16 May
> AGM. Short papers by Pastor E. H. Schaar, Hull German Lutheran Church, *The Ecumenical Character of Lutheranism,* and the Revd. H. C. West, Vicar of Sculcoates, Hull, *Christian Mission in the Secular City.*

Wednesday, 7 June
> Fr. Laurence Bright O.P. (in place of the Revd. Prof. C. Davis, Heythrop College), *The Nature of Faith.* Joint Newman Circle and Theological Society meeting.

The Second Decade

Though struggling with cash-flow problems and vacillating membership, the Society gained strength through co-operation with like-minded organisations, where a pooling of audiences must have considerably invigorated the proceedings – a kind of symbiosis. Joint meetings with the Newman Circle and the Historical Association have already been mentioned and the programame card for 1966-1967 carries a notice of a joint meeting of the Classical and Hellenic Associations on 20 January 1967, at which Prof. A. Wasserstein, of Leicester University, was to speak on *Philo the Jew*. This was obviously intended to encourage Theological Society members to lend their support.

The next AGM took place on 10 May 1968, after what must have been a particularly ambitious and varied season, starting with lectures on Buddhism, Islam and Judaism, and with a talk on the Eastern Orthodox Church still to come. Although it had not yet proved possible to recruit a Jewish representative to the committee, the Communal Rabbi, Dr Chaim J. Cooper, was evidently giving the Society his full support, as this was his second visit.

The opening lecture given by the High Commissioner for Ceylon (Sri Lanka) in the Middleton Hall was clearly an important occasion, meriting Press coverage: a pencilled note on the card gives the name 'Taylor Shaw' and the telephone number of the *Hull Daily Mail*. Mr Shaw was one of the senior reporters at that time, and it would appear that it was he who was charged with the duty of recording the event. The Society also seemed to be making more of the 'Student Evenings': for the first time, the speakers, Eamon Duffy and Jennifer Keron, were named and their subjects given.

The AGM could not, of course, ignore the mundane but necessary matters of finance and elections. The Treasurer reported that the switch from 'Room 16' to the Lecture Theatre had achieved the desired result of reducing costs, but he reiterated his plea for more subscribing members.*

---

*It is not clear how this reduction in costs was achieved, since the annual accounts at this stage do not show any charge for the hire of accommodation. Indeed, in the minutes of the 1987 AGM, 19 years later, the Secretary, J. L. North, calls attention to the Society's indebtedness to the University, the Department of Theology and the committee, 'by whose kind offices, over and above the call of duty, the membership subscription was kept so low'. The cost of the meeting room, of entertainment and overnight accommodation of speakers, of postages, telephoning and printing were never charged to the Society, he added. It is possible that a heating charge may have been payable for some rooms and not for others, but this does not show up on the accounts. Members sometimes offered overnight hospitality to visiting speakers. In 1968, 'Room 16' – or 'S16' – was in what was then the Social Sciences Building and is now named the Wilberforce Building. 'The Lecture Theatre' presumably refers to one of the theatres in the newly-constructed Arts Building, now the Larkin Building.

Vice-Presidents, Secretary, Treasurer and Auditor were re-elected, and Miss S. Clithero joined the committee as student representative, replacing Mr W. T. Hicks. The meeting approved the list of prospective speakers for the next session, then listened to papers read by Mrs M. Shorter and the Revd. F. G. Hunter.

PROGRAMME 1967-1968

Tuesday, 17 October, 1967
> H. E. The High Commissioner for Ceylon (Sri Lanka), Sir Lalita Rajapikse, *The Buddha and his Teaching.* Meeting held in the Middleton Hall, starting at 8 pm.

Tuesday, 7 November
> Mr Talal Asad, Department of Sociology, Hull University, *Islam in the Modern World.*

Tuesday, 5 December
> The Revd. Dr Chaim J. Cooper, Communal Rabbi of Hull, *The Worship of the Synagogue.*

Friday, 19 January, 1968
> Prof. A. M Armstrong, Professor of Greek, Liverpool University, *Platonic and Christian Love.* (Joint meeting with the Hull Classical Association).

Friday, 26 January
> Students from the Department of Theology, Hull University. Mr Eamon Duffy, *A Theology of Death,* and Miss Jennifer C. Keron, *Goethe's Religious Thought.*

Friday, 23 February
> Dr John A. Watt, Senior Lecturer in History, Hull University, *Church and State from Vatican I to Vatican II.*

Friday, 26 April
> The Very Revd. Dr Alan Richardson, Dean of York, *The Idea of Orthodoxy.*

Friday, 10 May
> AGM. Short papers by the Revd. F. G. Hunter, Vicar of St Martin, Hull, *Apologetics in the Parish,* and Mrs Mary Shorter, *The Virgin Birth and the Fourth Gospel.*

Running smoothly

The 1968-1969 programme appears to have run smoothly, and the fact that the majority of the speakers were local probably accounts for the ability of Mr Baslington to report 'a slightly increased balance-in-hand of £7.2s.6d.' at the AGM on 30 April 1969. All the officers were re-elected, and the only changes in the committee were that Mr Keith Wilkinson replaced Miss S. Clithero as student representative and the Revd. F. G. Hunter was elected in place of the Revd. D. Carter.

The printed card for the previous year indicates that it had originally been planned for Archbishop Anthony Bloom, Metropolitan of Sourozh, to give a lecture on *Orthodox Spirituality* at the end of that session 5 June, 1968, at a joint meeting with Hull Newman Circle, but evidently this was postponed until the start of the next session on 16 October, 1968. Speakers at the Annual General Meeting were Dr Elfride Bickersteth and Fr. A. J. Storey. The card indicates that the Bishop of Hull was originally to have spoken but no doubt pressure of duties must have obliged him to withdraw.

At this stage, the Society was apparently switching the venue between Lecture Theatre D and Room S16, according to which best suited the occasion. In fact, the growing number of alternative meeting places recorded – including Room S14 in the Social Sciences and Law Building and Room 131 in the Earth Sciences Building – may reflect the large developments then taking place on the University campus.

PROGRAMME 1968-1969

Wednesday, 16 October, 1968
  The Most Revd. Anthony Bloom, Metropolitan of Sourozh, *Orthodox Spirituality*.
Friday, 15 November
  Dr Malcolm Easton, Senior Lecturer in the History of Art, Hull University, *Rembrandt's Religious Art* (Illustrated).
Friday, 6 December
  The Revd. Dr. R. N. Whybray, Lecturer in Theology, Hull University, *Myth and Ritual and the Old Testament*.
Friday, 17 January, 1969
  Prof. F. F. Bruce, Rylands Professor of Biblical Exegesis, Manchester University, *Paul – Roman Citizen*. (Joint meeting with Hull Classical Association).
Friday, 14 February
  Students' Evening. Papers will be read by student members of the Department of Theology, Hull University.
Friday, 14 March
  Prof. Arthur Pollard, Professor of English, Hull University, *William Cowper, Evangelical Poet*.
Friday, 25 April (date changed to Wednesday, 30 April)
  AGM. Speakers, Dr Elfride Bickersteth, *Chasing the Words of the Greek Fathers,* and the Revd. Fr. A. J. Storey, *Authority and Doctrine in the Catholic Church*.
Friday, 9 May
  Dr. H. F. Mathews, Principal, Summerfield College, Kidderminster, *Current Trends in Religious Education* (Joint meeting with the Institute of Education Hull University).

More changes

During the 1970s, the minutes become very short and businesslike, and most of the activities of the Society are reflected in the programme cards and leaflets, but the records of the Annual General Meetings still provide useful information about those two related factors, membership and money, and put names to those who served on the committee or as officers. On 14 May 1970, the Treasurer reported a slightly increased balance of £9.6s.10d., 'mainly due to increased student subscriptions (19 against five the previous year)' – a welcome trend. In view of the tendency, mentioned above, for young students to hive off into their own groups, one may perhaps hazard a guess that the number of student members of the Society at any given time may be affected by the number of mature students coming into the department. Theology is, of course, a subject which attracts older people, including ordained ministers seeking to improve their qualifications. Miss P. A. Stobart was elected student representative in place of Mr K. H. Wilkinson, and Mr Kevin Harrison was also elected to the committee. Papers were read by Mr Kerry Holroyd and the Revd. Tegwyn Francis.

* * * *

On 13 May 1971, Mr Baslington reported a healthy state of affairs, with a balance of £18, due to a larger number of subscriptions, plus the profit from the showing at the November meeting of Pasolini's 'The Gospel According to St. Matthew', described as 'simply the best biblical film ever made'. 'While speakers' expenses were greater than in other years, income was also larger, the Treasurer pointed out. It is perhaps worth noting that the season had opened with the first Guru Nanak Memorial Lecture given by Dr. Aujla, presumably the Society's first Sikh speaker. Miss Ann Eccleston was elected student representative in place of Miss P. A. Stobart, and Dr J. E. Bickersteth and Mrs A. J. Bruce also joined the committee. The speakers of the evening were Mr Clifford Freeman and the Revd. Gordon O'Loughlin.

PROGRAMME 1969-1970

Friday, 17 October, 1969
   Prof. Sean O'Riordan, C.SS.R., Professor in the Lateran University, Rome, *New Trends in Christian Morals*.

Friday, 14 November
   The Revd. L. W. Barnard, Lecturer in Theology, Leeds University, *The Logos Theology of St Justin Martyr* (Joint meeting with the Classical Association).

Friday, 5 December
   Dr P. A. M. Taylor, Senior Lecturer in American Studies, Hull University, *The Early Mormons, Their History and Beliefs*.

Thursday, 22 January, 1970
> The Revd . Prof. R. P. C. Hanson, Professor of Christian Theology Nottingham University, *The Historicity of Acts.*

Thursday, 5 February
> Students' Evening. Mr Patrick Brain, *Religion as the Inexpressible,* and Mr David Pike, *Christian Baptism – an Examination.*

Thursday, 26 February
> Mr John M. Todd, of Messrs Darton, Longman and Todd, *The Reformation in Perspective.*

Thursday, 5 March
> The Lord Abbot of Ampleforth, the Rt. Revd. Dom Basil Hume, O.S.B., *Searching for God.*

Thursday, 23 April
> Dr Alistair A. Kee, Lecturer in Theology, Hull University, *Camilo Torres and Helder Camara: Catholic Revolutionaries.*

Thursday, 14 May
> AGM. The Revd. Tegwyn Francis, *Christianity and Ethics,* and Mr Kerry Holroyd, *Some Personal Reflections on Eschatology.*

PROGRAMME 1970-1971

Wednesday, 21 October, 1970
> Dr. Aujla, *The Guru Nanak.* First Guru Nanak Memorial Lecture.

Thursday, 12 November
> Film, Pasolini's 'The Gospel According to St. Matthew'. (Held in the University Lecture Theatre.)

Thursday, 3 December
> Dr A .J. Michie, Senior Lecturer in English Literature, Hull University, *Tragic Vision and the Christian Faith.*

Friday, 15 January, 1971
> Prof. J. B. Skemp, Professor of Greek, Durham University, *The Earliest Greek Christians – The 'Greeks' of the New Testament* (Joint meeting with Hull Branch of the Classical Association).

Thursday, 4 February
> The Revd. John J. Vincent, Director of the Urban Theology Unit, *The Liberated Church.*

Thursday, 18 February
> Student Evening: Mr Heward Wilkinson, *Being, Myth and Religion,* and Miss Alexandra Naismith, *The Spiritual Gifts of the New Testament and the Church Today.*

Thursday, 6 May
> The Revd. Prof. Peter Ackroyd, Professor of Old Testament, King's College, London University, *The Theology of Tradition.*

Thursday, 13 May
> AGM. Mr Clifford Freeman, *An Anglican View of East Riding*

Methodism a Century Ago, and the Revd. Gordon O'Loughlin, Vicar of St Alban, Hull, *The Gospels and the Pulpit.*

Pounds and Pence

On 10 May 1972, Treasurer Baslington was able to repeat the phrase 'a healthy state of affairs', with a balance of £24.29, due to increased subscriptions from both full members and students, 'though the increase in speakers' expenses was also to be noted'. This was the first balance sheet to show the figures in decimal currency, introduced in 1971, and both this and Britain's entry into the Common Market (EU) two years later had the effect of inflating figures generally, though this did not necessarily reflect a particular financial situation, individual or corporate: income and expenditure both appeared to rise. Mr M. R. Haines was elected student representative in place of Miss Ann Eccleston, Mr J. Lyons was elected in place of Sister Mary Richard, and Mr C. M. Price in place of the Revd. F. G. Hunter. Miss Judith Secret was elected to the committee, and also read a paper to the Society. A second paper was read by the Revd. R. H. Darroch.

* * * *

Thursday, 10 May 1973, saw the last presentation of the accounts by Mr Baslington, who had looked after the Society's cash since 1964, and had steered it through difficult times. He was thanked very warmly for his work over the years – but there is no mention of a parting gift: the balance-in-hand was a creditable £21.63, but expenses had, of course, risen proportionately, so there was no room for largesse! Mrs Catherine Goulder was elected Treasurer in his place *, and Mr John Verity succeeded Mr M.R.Haines as student representative.

The year under review had brought to the platform the customary succession of distinguished academics, and this time the Student Evening had taken the form of a debate, 'Theology, Revolution and the Third World' – the first reference in the Society's records to this new term for the less-developed countries. The AGM concluded with papers read by the Revd. Donald Dugard and Mr Kevin Harrison.

* * * *

On 8 May 1974 Mrs Goulder, making her first report as Treasurer, announced a balance of £33.60. She was re-elected, along with the two Vice-Presidents and the Secretary. Mr Baslington joined the committee, together with the Revd. Dr. J. W. McKay, to replace Dr Whybray, and Miss

---

*Mrs Goulder, known to her colleagues as 'Kate', is currently the Revd. Catherine H. Goulder, Priest in charge of the Benefice of North Cave with Cliffe, held in plurality with Hotham, covering the churches of All Saints, North Cave, St John, North Cliffe, and St Oswald, Hotham.

Heather Farr, to replace Mr John Verity as student representative.

Speakers of the evening were Pastor E. L. Schnellbächer and Mr Philip Atkinson.

PROGRAMME 1971-1972

Thursday, 28 October, 1971
    The Revd. Prof. James Atkinson, Department of Biblical Studies, Sheffield University, *Luther 1521-1971: Debate with Rome.*

Friday, 12 November
    The Rt. Revd. Ian Ramsay, Lord Bishop of Durham, *Difficulties in Talking of God's Presence.*

Thursday, 2 December
    Prof. W. H. C. Frend, Professor of Ecclesiastical History, Glasgow University, *Heresy and Nationalism in the Early Church.*

Wednesday, 19 January, 1972
    Mr Robert Marchant Director of Music and Head of Department of Music, Hull University, *Christianity and the Shaping of Western Music.* (Illustrated).

Thursday, 10 February
    The Revd. Fr. Anthony Storey, Catholic Chaplain, Hull University, *Mary in the Theology of the Catholic Church.*

Thursday, 2 March
    Student Evening. Miss Marion Whatling, *The Early Christians and Classical Education,* and Mr John Dickason, *Community and Mission.*

Tuesday, 2 May
    The Revd. J. W. McKay, Lecturer in Theology, Hull University, *The Heresy of William Robertson Smith.*

Wednesday, 10 May
    AGM. Miss Judith Secret, *Archbishop Holgate and the Reformation in Yorkshire,* and the Revd. R. H. Darroch, *Bonhoeffer the Barthian.*

PROGRAMME 1972-1973

Tuesday, 24 October, 1972
    Prof. Geoffrey Parrinder, Professor of Comparative Religion, King's College, London, *Doctrines of Salvation: Christian Attitudes to Other Religions.*

Friday, 17 November
    Prof. H. D. Lewis, Professor of the Philosophy of Religion, King's College, London, *Life after Death.*

Thursday, 7 December
    Prof. Kathleen Jones, Professor of Social Administration and Social Work, York University, *Towards a Theology of Social Action.*

Tuesday, 16 January, 1973
   The Revd. John Rogerson, Lecturer in Theology, Durham University, *Hebrew Origins – Bedouin or Babylonian? A new look at an important methodological issue.*
Wednesday, 7 February
   Student Evening: Debate on 'Theology, Revolution and the Third World'. Miss Ruth Carrotte, Mr Jonathan Barry.
Wednesday, 21 February
   Prof. Rudolph Schnackenburg, Professor of New Testament, Würzburg University, *The Farewell Discourses in John.*
Thursday, 1 March
   Prof. A. F. Norman, Professor of Classics, Hull University, *Julian the Apostate – Reformer or Reactionary?*
Thursday, 10 May
   AGM. The Revd. Donald Dugard, *The Holy Spirit in the Gospel of St. John,* and Mr Kevin Harrison, *A Century of Hull Methodism.*

PROGRAMME 1973-1974

Tuesday, 16 October, 1973
   Prof D. M. McKay, Professor of Communications, Keele University, *Prayer in an Age of Science.*
Thursday, 29 November
   The Revd. Vernon Sproxton, BBC Television Producer, *The Religious Dynamics of Secular Broadcasting.*
Wednesday, 23 January, 1974
   Dr T. W. Bamford, Director, Institute of Education, Hull University, *Thomas Arnold and the Victorian Church.*
Tuesday, 12 February
   Annual Student Evening: Mr Colin Price, *Job and the Logical Positivists,* and Mr Mark Rye, *The Problem of Christian Individualism.*
Tuesday, 8 March
   The Revd Prof. E. J. Tinsley, Professor of Theology, Leeds University, *Theology and the Iconography of the Crucifixion* (Illustrated).
Wednesday, 8 May
   AGM. Pastor E. L. Schnellbächer. *A Short History of the German Lutheran Church in Hull,* and Mr Philip Atkinson, *Tertullian – Phrygian Montanist or North African Fanatic?*

Social Science
By the mid-1970s, the programmes had taken on a more soci--scientific flavour. At the Annual General Meeting on 14 May 1975, the Society was looking back on a season which had begun with a talk on *Religions of Asia and Social Development,* and had included lectures by a Professor of Genetics and a Professor of Psychiatry, and was looking forward to an

end-of-term address by the University's Lecturer in Chemistry. This programme had obviously been relatively expensive – speakers' expenses had totalled £50.15 – but the balance-in-hand, £16.93, was still on the right side of the ledger. Miss H. M. Farr and Mrs W. Sproston were elected to the committee, and Miss A. R. Dunkley was chosen to represent the students.

Business accomplished, papers were read by Dr John Biggs and Prof. L. H. C Thomas.

* * * *

It had to happen . . . On 10 May 1976, the AGM decided that 'because of the high cost of speakers' travelling expenses', subscriptions must rise to 80p per annum for full membership and 40p for students — still an incredibly modest charge for such a glittering series of lectures by leading theological scholars and writers. All the officers were re-elected, and Sister Alexia Morris joined the committee, along with Mrs Patricia Batstone as student representative. Papers were read by Sister Kira Solhdoost and the Revd. L. R. Pepper.

* * * *

The Faculty of Arts Meeting Room was the location of the 1976-1977 session, and at the AGM on 10 May 1977, members were able to reflect on a programme which was well up to standard, with Richard Hanson and Bishop Michael Ramsey making return visits. The Society ended the year with £26.58 in hand, and the Treasurer, Catherine Goulder, was re-elected along with the other officers. The Revd. E. Langdon replaced Miss J. L. Secret on the committee and Miss A. L. Davies was elected student representative. Papers were read by Mrs W. Sproston and Mr D. Kennedy.

PROGRAMME 1974-1975

Wednesday, 23 October, 1974
   Prof. Trevor Ling, Professor of Comparative Religion, Manchester University, *Religions of Asia and Social Development.*

Wednesday, 13 November
   The Revd. R. E. Clements, Fellow of Fitzwilliam College, and Lecturer in Old Testament, Cambridge University, *The Theological Significance of Sacrifice.*

Tuesday, 3 December
   Prof. D. A. Jones. Professor of Genetics, Hull University, *Man, the Experimental Animal.*

Tuesday, 28 January, 1975
   Mr Edward Hulmes, Director, Religious Studies Project, Farmington Trust, Oxford, *The Future of an Illusion: a Critique of Religious Education Orthodoxy.*

Tuesday, 18 February
> Prof. D. A. Pond Professor of Psychiatry, London Hospital Medical College, London University, *Public Ritual and Private Counselling.*

Tuesday, 11 March
> Annual Student Evening: Miss Maura Ring, *Zwingli – a First Generation Reformer* and Miss Wendy Symes, *The Alienation of Man.*

Wednesday, 14 May
> AGM. Dr John Biggs, Lecturer in Chemistry, Hull University, *Union or Unity?* and Prof. L. H . C. Thomas, Hull University, *Story or Sermon? – Jeremias Gotthelf.*

PROGRAMME 1975-1976

Thursday, 16 October, 1975
> The Very Revd. Eric Heaton, Dean of Durham, *The Birth of Biblical Literature.*

Tuesday, 18 November
> Prof. E. C. Fudge, Professor of Linguistics, Hull University, *The Interpretation of Texts – can Linguistics help?*

Monday, 1 December
> Dr P. J. Fitzpatrick, Lecturer in Philosophy, Durham University, *'Give me where to stand' – a Roman Catholic takes stock.*

Wednesday, 21 January, 1976
> Miss Eva Pinthus, Senior Lecturer, Department of Religious Studies, City of Leeds and Carnegie College of Education, *Discretion and Valour – some complexities of Christian Witness in Eastern Germany.*

Tuesday, 17 February
> Dr J. C. Thewlis, Lecturer in History, Hull University, *The Reintroduction of Papal Authority in England under Queen Mary.*

Tuesday, 9 March
> Annual Student Evening. Mr Michael More, *Religion and Evidence,* and Miss Ruth Collis, *Martin Bucer – 'The very model of a modern ecumenical'.*

Tuesday, 10 May
> AGM. Sister Kira Solhdoost, Endsleigh College of Education, *Explorations in Worship since Vatican II,* and the Revd. L. R. Pepper, *The Assumption of the Blessed Virgin Mary in Anglican Theology.*

PROGRAMME 1976-1977

Wednesday, 20 October, 1976
> Fr. Martin Jarret-Kerr, Community of the Resurrection, Mirfield, Associate Lecturer, Leeds University, *Frontier Treaties – English Literature and the Borders of Theology.*

Tuesday, 16 November
> Prof. the Rt. Revd. Richard Hanson, Professor of Historical Theology,

Manchester University, *The Relation of Christian Faith to History.*

Thursday, 2 December

The Very Revd. Dr Ernest Nicholson, Dean of Pembroke College, Cambridge, and University Lecturer in Old Testament, *The Decalogue as the Direct Address of God.*

Tuesday, 25 January, 1977

Annual Student Evening. Miss Sally Wormald, *Newman and Kingsley – Men of their Times?* and Mr John Wilde, *Betrayers or Betrayed? – the Anabaptists and the Reformation.*

Wednesday, 16 February

The Revd. Fr. Gabriel Daly, Irish School of Ecumenics and Augustinian House of Studies, Dublin, *Some Classical and Romantic Trends in Theology.*

Friday, 4 March

Bishop Michael Ramsey, *St John and the Holy Spirit.*

Tuesday, 10 May

AGM. Mrs Wendy Sproston, *The Johannine Christ,* and Mr David Kennedy, *The Challenge Presented by the Person of Sri Ramakrishna.*

The Third Decade

The Society began its third decade with a full programme of seven meetings, all held in the Faculty of Arts Meeting Room. At the AGM on 16 May 1978, the Treasurer reported a balance of £25.71, but in view of rising costs it was felt necessary to make another small adjustment to subscriptions. Full membership now cost £1 per annum and students paid 50p. The Revd. Ieuan P. Ellis retired with the thanks of the Society for his 12 years of service as Secretary, and was replaced by Mr Frank Lyons. Miss H. M. Last was elected to the committee as student representative and all the other members were re-elected. Mrs Goulder doubled her role as Treasurer by giving one of the two papers of the evening, the other being delivered by the Revd. Michael Buss.

* * * *

The Revd. Patrick J. Thompson slips from the records in 1979. There is no recorded valedictory tribute, which seems rather strange, because he had been a founder member, and had served as joint Vice-President since the office was created in 1963. However, it is understood that at the time of his retirement he was out of the country, on family business in Spain, so the expressions of appreciation were probably made privately. His co-Vice-President, Mr C.B. Freeman, was re-elected at the AGM on 8 May 1979, and from that time onward the Society had only one VP. The Revd. F. Myhill was elected to the committee in place of the Revd. E. Langdon, Miss Susanne Tree became the new student representative, and it was suggested that Mr David Cherry should be invited to join the committee should Sister Alexia Morris not be able to attend meetings. The Treasurer reported a balance of £46.16, due, it would seem, to a steep rise in membership, the subscription figures indicating 39 full members and 37 students. Readers of the evening were the Revd. Michael Smith and the Revd. Philip Rigby.

It must have been a source of satisfaction, not only to active feminists, but to the membership generally, to observe the increasing number of women taking part in the life of the Society, both as organisers and as speakers – a feature of which the Society can be proud. This no doubt reflected the rising number of girls able – and willing – to enter higher education; and, though the ordination of women into the Church of England was still some way off, it was gratifying to see, in a materialistic world, so many people attracted to the study of Theology, the Queen of Sciences!

PROGRAMME 1977-1978

Tuesday, 25 October, 1977
  The Very Revd. Ronald Jasper, Dean of York, *Building up the Body of Christ*.
Tuesday, 15 November
  Dom Henry Wansbrough, Ampleforth Abbey, *The Jesus Myth*.
Tuesday, 6 December
  Dr Ronald Paterson, Department of Adult Education, Hull University, *The Problem of Evil*.
Wednesday, 25 January, 1978
  Bishop Kenneth Cragg, Reader in Religious Studies, Sussex University, *Meeting in Meaning – a Mediating Theology*.
Tuesday, 14 February
  Annual Student Evening, Mr Gerald Beauchamp, *A Theology of History*, and Mr Graham Lewis, *Aquinas' Converter – or Transforming Belief into Faith*.
Thursday, 9 March
  The Revd. Patrick Vaughan, Vicar of Hovingham, *The Archaeology of Jerusalem* (illustrated).
Tuesday, 16 May,
  AGM. Mrs Catherine Goulder, *Moral Theology in the 17th Century*, and the Revd. Michael Buss, Kingston Reformed Church, *The Forgotten Owen, the Puritan Vice-Chancellor of Oxford*.

PROGRAMME 1978-1979

Tuesday, 24 October, 1978
  The Revd. Prof. John Macquarrie, Lady Margaret Professor of Divinity, Oxford University, *Christianity and Other Faiths*.
Thursday, 9 November
  Dr James Dunn, Department of Theology, Nottingham University, *The Author of Acts – Early Catholic or Enthusiast?*
Wednesday, 6 December
  The Revd. Dr Hans Wijngaards, Vicar General, Mill Hill Missionaries, *The Church and Scripture – with special reference to some topical questions*.
Tuesday, 23 January, 1979
  Prof. V. A. McClelland, Professor of Educational Studies, Hull University, *Newman: a Study in Limitations*.
Tuesday, 13 February
  Dr D. L. Gosling, Department of Theology, Hull University, *Nuclear Theology*.
Tuesday, 6 March
  -Students' Evening. Mr Anthony Purvis, *Theology as Grammar?* and Mr Christopher Cook, *Christ and Buddha*.

Tuesday, 8 May
> AGM. The Revd. Michael Smith, Chaplain of Pocklington School, *Liberty or Licence? – the long-term effect of James II's Declaration of Indulgence on the pastoral ministry of the Church of England,* and the Revd. Philip Rigby, Methodist Chaplain to Hull University, *Poetry and Piety – Theology in the Wesleys' Hymns.*

Top names

The Society's minute-book may be short on detail at this period, but the list of speakers for 1979-1980 indicates that the season must have started in great style with a visit from Prof. Ninian Smart, a prolific writer whose involvement with the BBC's television programme, 'The Long Search' and Radio 3 series, 'The Long Search Continued' introduced many viewers and listeners to world religions.

At the AGM on 7 May 1980, Mrs Wendy Sproston was elected Vice-President and Mr M. Priestman joined the committee as student representative. The Treasurer reported a balance of £58.71. Papers were read by Dr Louis Billington and the Revd. D.Young.

From 1980, some correspondence files become available, giving interesting insights into what was going on in the background. According to a letter from President Anthony Hanson to the Secretary, Frank Lyons, on 8 May 1980, the AGM readers had not realised that each was meant to produce a half-paper: 'In effect, each read a full paper, both very good, but it meant that we ran very late.'

* * * *

Lined up for the 1980-1981 session were, among others: the Roman Catholic Bishop of Middlesbrough, Augustine Harris, the Dean of Durham, the Very Revd. Peter Baelz, and Hull University's Professor of Politics, Dr. C. H. Dodd, while the Annual Student Evening indicated an intriguing gender-twist, Susanne Tree speaking on *Theology in Practice* and Jonathan Parker on *Feminist Theology.*

An exchange of letters between Prof. Hanson and Prof. Mackey over expenses also makes amusing reading: 'Second class fare plus one lunch from British Rail cost me in all £36.80 which more than persuaded me to travel by car in future, however much trouble it may be!' wrote the canny Scot, adding, 'But I was delighted to meet the theological community at Hull and sorry only that my ignorance of time limits deprived me of more of its theological comment on my rather rangy talk. But perhaps I can lick the second one into shape and send it to you for comment.' In his letter of thanks, Prof. Hanson said, 'I should be most interested to see your lecture in written form. I am sure it is worth working on' – a somewhat left-handed compliment, perhaps. (The subject of Caledonian thrift crops up again in a letter dated 16 February 1992 from Dr David

Jasper, who wrote, 'A mercenary point. Can I claim some help for travel? Otherwise, I shall need to claim from Glasgow – a very complicated business in Scotland!')

By the date of the AGM on 7 May 1981, the balance-in-hand was £28.56, and thanks were expressed to Treasurer Kate and to Mrs Sproston for auditing the accounts.

The officers were all re-elected and new names appearing on the committee list were Mr J. Betts, Miss M. M. Henson and Mr A. Milligan.

Business ended, a paper was read by Mr J. Bernasconi.

Elusive Primate

Pinning down Archbishop Stuart Blanch seems to have been a lengthy operation, as His Grace was a great traveller. Correspondence began in June 1978, when Domestic Chaplain Bob Lewis wrote to the Society Secretary, Ieuan Ellis, 'You offered plenty of dates, but I am afraid to say that none of them is any good. In view of the clogged state of next autumn, I think His Grace would hope rather to come in the following term i.e. January-March 1980. It is a long way ahead, and we cannot put definite dates in yet, but if you were able to give me some suggestions, together with the dates of the term, that would take us some way and then we could work it out later when other recurring fixtures are known.' And in February 1979, the chaplain wrote to Ieuan Ellis's successor, Frank Lyons, 'I have all the correspondence ready to discuss with the Archbishop when he gets back from South India next month.' A booking was made for 31 January 1980, and a title chosen, *Jesus the Rabbi,* but fate was to intervene in the shape of an illness. On 21 February 1980, Dr Blanch wrote, 'Thank you very much for your card and for the best wishes of the Theological Society. I was particularly sorry to miss the engagement because it would have been nice to have met you all, but I think I would have been distinctly less than coherent and that would have been a pity.' The long-awaited talk finally took place on 25 November 1982. In a letter to Frank Lyons dated 25 February 1982, the Archbishop wrote, 'I shall probably regret the title, *Jesus the Rabbi,* but I will do my best with it.'

PROGRAMME 1979-1980

Thursday, 18 October, 1979
 Prof. Ninian Smart, Professor of Religious Studies, Lancaster University, *Buddhism, Christianity and Personal Identity.*
Wednesday, 7 November
 The Revd. Prof. Barnabas Lindars, SSF, Rylands Professor of Biblical Criticism and Exegesis, Manchester University, *Enoch and Christology.*
Thursday, 6 December
 The Revd. Prof. David Jenkins, Professor of Theology and Religious

Studies, Leeds University, *Reflections on the Nature and Methods of Theology.*
(Thursday, 31 January, 1980 Postponed)
The Archbishop of York, Dr Stuart Blanch, *Jesus the Rabbi.*
Tuesday, 19 February
Dr Daniel Mariau, Department of Theology, Hull University, *Indian Christian Theology.-*
Tuesday, 11 March
Student Evening. Mr Glyn Holland, *Dostoevsky – Prophet of our Time?* and Miss Mary Huston, *The Turin Shroud – a Fifth Gospel.*
(A handwritten note suggests that Dr R. N. Whybray gave a talk on 18 March)
Wednesday, 7 May
AGM. Dr L. Billington, Department of American Studies, Hull University, *Folk Beliefs and Popular Evangelism in Early 19th-Century England,* and the Revd. D. Young, Vicar of Patrington, *F. D. Maurice.*

PROGRAMME 1980-1981

Wednesday, 22 October, 1980
Prof. J. P. Mackey, Professor of Divinity, Edinburgh University, *Christian Faith and Common History.*
Tuesday, 18 November
Dr J. F. A. Sawyer, Head of the Department of Religious Studies, Newcastle University, *Biblical Language in Context.*
Wednesday, 3 December
Prof. C. H. Dodd, Professor of Politics, Hull University, *The Political Role of the Shi'ite Clergy in Iran.*
January, 1981
Bishop Augustine Harris, Bishop of Middlesbrough (date and time to be announced).
Tuesday, 10 February
Annual Student Evening. Susanne Tree, *Theology in Practice,* and Jonathan Parker, *Feminist Theology.*
Monday, 2 March
The Very Revd. Peter Baelz, Dean of Durham, one-time Regius Professor of Moral and Pastoral Theology, Oxford University, *The Ethical and the Pastoral – Convergence or Conflict?* (Joint Religious Education Association and Theological Society meeting held at Inglemire Avenue site of Hull College of Higher Education).
Wednesday, 18 March
Prof. N. L. A. Lash, Norris-Hulse Professor of Divinity, Cambridge University, *Standards of Orthodoxy.*

Thursday, 7 May
AGM. Mr J. Bernasconi, Hon. Curator, University Art Collection, Hull University, *Miraculous Paintings of the Renaissance.*

Farewell

Before members met for the AGM on 6 May 1982, they had said farewell to Prof. Anthony Hanson, who had led the Society as President for 20 years. Again, there are no recorded tributes but there is no doubt that it was due to his considerable influence that so many distinguished scholars had been persuaded to visit the City – for little or no monetary reward. He had left a splendid legacy.

Prof. Hanson was succeeded by the Revd. Ieuan P. Ellis, and the annual meeting saw what in political terms might be described as a Cabinet Reshuffle: Mrs Sproston remained as Vice-President, Mr J. L. North was elected Secretary (he received his Doctorate in 1989), and Mr Lyons moved over to take charge of the Exchequer. The committee now consisted of Dr Elfride Bickersteth, Miss M. M. Henson, the Revd. F. Myhill and Fr. A. J. Storey.

The Treasurer reported a balance of £23.09 'which reflected a successful year's programme', but inflation was creeping up on even the most economically-run organisations, so subscriptions were increased to £1.50 for full membership and 75p for students.

Speaker of the evening was the Revd. Michael M. Hennell, Canon of Manchester Cathedral. Perhaps the committee had realised, after the occasion of the over-running essayists, that one well-presented paper was sufficient to fill the time available after the business meeting.

* * * *

Another fine series of lectures was reviewed at the AGM on 4 May 1983, starting with a return visit by the Rt. Revd. Prof. R. P. C. Hanson. As already recorded, the Society had been due for a Patronal visit by the Archbishop of York, Dr Stuart Blanch, in January 1980, but this had to be postponed on account of the Primate's illness, and the visit did not take place until 25 November 1982. When Dr Eamon Duffy returned to his *Alma Mater* in December 1982, he was roped in for extra duties by President Ellis: 'Will you have time to address Third and Second Year students on Tuesday morning 7 December, at 11.15 on some topic connected with 19th-century Catholicism (or, indeed, any 19th-century topic you would like to talk about)?' he wrote. 'It would be very good for them to hear a voice from outside the Department on Victorian church history – and it would be a tonic for me! Do say you can do it.' There is no reply on file, but how could the young scholar resist such blandishments? In any case, he was apparently 'staying over' with his friends, the Goulders, so he had no excuse. The AGM ratified the subscription increases, and agreed to charge 50p for those attending 'isolated' meetings; approved the draft programme for the following year; and then listened to a reading by the Secretary, J. Lionel North.

PROGRAMME 1981-1982

Thursday, 22 October, 1981
   B. McSweeney, Irish School of Economics, *The Church as Critic*.

Tuesday, 10 November
   Prof. C. H. Dodd, Professor of Politics, Hull University, *The Revival of Islam in Modern Turkey*.

Thursday, 3 December
   D. J. A. Clines, Department of Biblical Studies, Sheffield University, *Holy Places, Sacred Space and Such Like*.

Monday, 18 January, 1982
   J. A. Williams, *Change or Decay: The Provincial Laity 1691-1781*.

Wednesday, 10 February
   Annual Student Evening. Speakers and titles to be announced.

Friday, 12 March
   Dr Margaret E. Thrall, Department of Biblical Studies, University College of North Wales, Bangor, *The Offender and the Offence, 2 Corinthians 2:5*.

Thursday, 6 May
   AGM. The Revd. Canon Michael M. Hennell, Canon of Manchester Cathedral, *Anglican Evangelicalism in the Generation after the Death of Wilberforce*.

PROGRAMME 1982-1983

Tuesday, 19 October, 1982
   The Rt. Rev. Prof. R. P. C. Hanson, Manchester University, *Whatever happened to Arius? (An inspection of the development of doctrine)*.

Thursday, 25 November
   The Most Revd Stuart Blanch, Archbishop of York, *Jesus the Rabbi*.

Monday, 6 December
   Dr Eamon Duffy, Director of Studies in History, Magdalene College, Cambridge, *Newton's Cosmos and the Church of England: A Seventeenth-Century Fairy Story*.

Tuesday, 18 January, 1983
   Dr Edmund Little, Hull University, *A Literary Critic Looks at the Gospels*.

Tuesday, 8 February
   The Rt. Revd. K. O'Brien, Auxiliary Bishop of Middlesbrough, *Mary the Mother of Jesus*.

March
   Annual Student Evening. Date, speakers and titles to be announced.

Wednesday, 4 May
AGM. Mr J. L. North, Hull University, *Paul's Appeals for Unity in Philippians: in honour of Hugo Grotius (1583-1645).*

Reformation

The year 1983 was special as it marked the 500th anniversary of the birth of Martin Luther, and the Society collaborated with the Department of Theology in spreading the celebrations throughout the County of Humberside – as it then was. In addition to the Society's own season of meetings, featuring some of the best-known theologians of the day, a number of additional lectures were arranged by the Department during November, the month of Luther's birth. These were to see a return of former staff members, Canon J. Atkinson and Prof. A. G. Dickens, together with Prof. B. Möller of Göttingen, and the Revd. Dr R. Brown, Principal of Spurgeon's College, London. Public lectures were to be delivered by the Revd. Dr. David S. Russell, President of the Baptist Union of Great Britain and Ireland, on 19 October and by Prof. James Barr, Regius Professor of Hebrew at Oxford University, on 27 October. Dr Russell was also to be the preacher at the University Service in the Middleton Hall on 19 October. 'Preparation for Christian Leadership' courses were run at the Methodist Central Hall in Hull and the Doughty Centre in Grimsby. These were intended for those already in positions of leadership within the Church – lay readers, local preachers and leaders of house groups, Mothers' Union, Sunday School and discussion groups, 'or for those who feel that they would profit from a course slanted in that direction'. These courses, organised by J. Lionel North, the Theological Society's Secretary, included Bible Study, Communicating the Faith, Church Structures (Grimsby), Luther (Hull) and Thomas à Kempis (Grimsby). In addition, a 20-week course on 'Human values in Industrial Society' was arranged by the Revd. Geoffrey Sturman at the University. It seems likely that the interest created by this county-wide programme boosted the fortunes of the Hull and District Theological Society, because at the AGM, on 3 May 1984, it was announced that membership now amounted to 57, and 'this, with the handsome credit balance (£41.90), was very encouraging'.

Three committee members, Dr J. E. Bickersteth, Mr John Day and the Revd. F. Myhill, tendered their resignations, which were received 'with regret and thanks for their service'. In their places, the Revd. David Atkinson and Miss D. A. Eccleston were elected and the President and Secretary were empowered to seek and appoint a student representative. Miss Leslie Bowman and Miss Karen Hodgson were 'most warmly thanked for their sterling work on behalf of the Society, especially as dispensers of biscuits, coffee and kindness!'

Suggestions were sought for themes and speakers for 1985-1986: the Archbishop of York and Prof. W. Hollenweger were among the names put forward, and possible themes were 'The Third World and Revolutionary Theology', 'The Right Wing Critique of Christian Comments on Social Issues', 'Narrative Exegesis' and '1886 as the year of birth of several famous German theologians'. A lecture by Dr L. L. Grabbe brought the meeting to a close. Perhaps it would be going a bit too far to say that 1983 was an *Annus Mirabilis* for the Society – but things certainly appeared to be looking up!

PROGRAMME 1983-1984

Wednesday, 26 October 1983
> The Revd. Prof. James Barr, Regius Professor of Hebrew, Oxford University, *Why the world was created in 4004 BC: Archbishop Ussher and Biblical Chronology.*

Monday, 28 November
> The Revd. Dr. C. K. Barrett, Emeritus Professor of Divinity, Durham University, *Paul's Voyage to Rome (Acts 27).*

Monday, 23 January, 1984
> The Very Revd. Dr Henry Chadwick, Regius Professor Emeritus of Divinity, Cambridge University, *The Distinctiveness and Originality of Early Christian Ethics.*

Monday, 20 February
> Students' Evening. *The Future of Church Ministry.* Speakers, Dominic Anderson, John Day, Duncan Johnston. Chairman, Ian Watts.

Wednesday, 14 March
> Prof. Michael Pye, Marburg University, West Germany, *Interpreting Japanese Religion.*

Thursday, 3 May
> AGM. Dr L. L. Grabbe, *Revolutionaries, Sects, Sons of Abraham: Judaism in the First Century.*

Encouraging

The tide of success was still running when members met for the AGM on 2 May 1985. Subscription figures indicated a paid-up membership of 66 (43 'ordinary' members plus 23 students), an increase of nine over the previous year. So the Secretary was able to repeat his verdict: 'This, with the handsome credit balance, was very encouraging.' Cash in the bank was, in fact, £53.82 and again one is struck by the contrast between the intellectual weight of the speakers and their erudite subjects and the financial shoestring which was making their presence possible. The meeting accepted with regret the resignation of Father Anthony Storey, and Mr Dominic Anderson was elected in his place. The Revd. (later Revd. Dr) Peter Stubley also joined the committee. It seemed that there had been a wedding since the last annual meeting – Miss M. M. Henson was now Mrs Margaret Flood. The accounts were audited by Mr M. M. Hughes. The draft programme for the following season was approved, with the comment that 'Systematic Theology should be represented more prominently in future!' A return visit by Prof. R. N. Whybray was also called for. To complete the evening's activity, a paper was read by Dom Patrick Barry, Abbot of Ampleforth – and discussion continued over the coffee-cups.

* * * *

At the AGM on 1 May 1986, however, attention was drawn to 'some decline in the Society's membership', which appears to have peaked in the mid-1980s with the Reformation celebrations, then dipped again. All the officers and committee members were re-elected – and there were no resignations. The draft programme for 1986-1987 was presented and approved. Dr Ursula King, of Leeds, was the speaker of the evening, and her talk was followed by 'discussion and coffee'.

PROGRAMME 1984-1985

Thursday, 18 October, 1984
    The Revd. Prof. Barnabas Lindars, SSF, Rylands Professor of Biblical Criticism and Exegesis, Manchester University, *The Sound of the Trumpet: Paul and Eschatology*.

Tuesday, 27 November
    Dr Alistair Kee, Head of Department of Religious Studies, Glasgow University, *Karl Marx's Proof of the Existence of God*.

Wednesday, 5 December
    Prof. Morna Hooker, Lady Margaret's Professor of Divinity, Cambridge University, *What are you doing here, Elijah? Another look at the Transfiguration story*.

Tuesday, 22 January, 1985
    Prof. Donald Earl, Professor of Classics, Hull University, *St Augustine and the Romanisation of Christianity*.

Wednesday, 20 February
    Dr Samuel Lieu, Department of Classical Civilisation, Warwick University, *The Holy Men in Early Byzantium and Medieval China*.

Thursday, 7 March
    Students' Evening. Jenny Sutton, Matthew Thompson and June Higginson will introduce papers on *Deification, Process Theology,* and *Judgement*. (Students encouraged to support).

Thursday, 2 May
    AGM. (The advertised speaker was Dom Ambrose Griffiths, OSB, Abbot Emeritus of Ampleforth Abbey, but, according to the minutes, Dom Patrick Barry, the current Abbot of Ampleforth, read a paper entitled *Monastic Vocation Today: Commitment, Community, Contemplation*).

The programme cards had now become more informative about the

Society, and were apparently being more widely used for publicity purposes. This, and the following card carry an extract from John Stuart Mill's inaugural address as Rector of St Andrews on 1 February 1867: *'To question all things – never to turn away from any difficulty; to accept no doctrine either from ourselves or from other people without a rigid scrutiny by negative criticism; letting no fallacy, no incoherence, or confusion of thought step by unperceived; above all, to insist upon having the meaning of a word clearly understood before using it, and the meaning of a proposition before assenting to it: – these are the lessons we learn from ancient dialecticians.'*

PROGRAMME 1985-1986

Wednesday, 23 October, 1985
    Dr P. M. Casey, Department of Theology, Nottingham University, *God Incarnate: Jesus in the Johannine Community.*

Thursday, 14 November
    The Revd. Prof R. N. Whybray, Emeritus Professor, Hull University, *Old Testament Theology – a Non-Existent Beast?*

Tuesday, 3 December
    Dr Jack Dominian, Consultant Psychiatrist, Central Middlesex Hospital, *Christian Marriage.*

Monday, 20 January, 1986
    Prof. B. Moloney, Professor of Italian, Hull University, Title to he announced.

Wednesday, 12 February
    Students' Evening. Speakers and titles to he announced.

Thursday, 13 March
    Fr. Anthony Storey, Cottingham, *Man and Woman in Scripture.*

Thursday, 1 May
    AGM. Dr Ursula King, Department of Theology and Religious Studies, Leeds University, *Spirituality and Contemporary Society: Some Explanations and Questions.*

Ups and Downs

The Treasurer's report presented at the AGM on 7 May 1987 showed that the 'handsome credit balance' had now shrunk to £22.69, but the Society was still solvent. And it was not the financial situation which caused concern but the standard of the refreshments! 'After scurrilous comments about the quality of the coffee, the statement was accepted,' state the minutes. The resignation of the President, the Revd. I. P. Ellis, and of the Revd. D. Atkinson were received with regret. The Secretary thanked them both for their service to the Society and called attention to the fact that Mr Ellis had served as Secretary for 16 years and as President for five years.

    Officers and committee elected, or re-elected, to lead the Society into its fourth decade were: President, Mrs W. E. Sproston; Vice-President, Dr L. L. Grabbe; Secretary, Mr J. L. North; Treasurer, Mr F. Lyons; committee, Mr D. Anderson, Miss A. Eccleston, Mrs M. M. Flood, Mrs J. Higginson, the Revd. P. D. Stubley and the Revd. A. J. Wells. It was at this meeting that the Secretary called attention to the Society's indebtedness to the University, the Department of Theology and members of the committee, to which reference has already been made. Business ended, Prof. Max Wilcox presented a paper entitled *Anna the Prophetess*. And at the concluding social session the coffee may not have been to everyone's taste but the discussion was doubtless champagne-sparkling.

PROGRAMME 1986-1987

There is no printed programme on file for the year 1986-1987, but there is an outline list of names and dates on the agenda for the 1986 AGM, and diary entries supplied by Dr J. Lionel North and Dr Elfride Bickersteth fill in further details:

20 October, 1986
  The Revd. Prof. A.T. Hanson, *Modern Ministry*.
13 November
  Dr Sheridan Gilley, *The Life of Cardinal Manning*.
2 December
  Dr Harry Parkin, *Bhakti* (In Hinduism, Devotional Self-Surrender to God).
27 January, 1987
  Dr Judith Lieu, *What did the New Testament Writers know about the Pharisees?*
26 February
  Students' Evening with Mary Bentall and Christine Hensell.
12 March
  Prof. Stephen Sykes, *Divine Omnipotence and Kenotic Trinitology*.
7 May
  AGM. Prof. Max Wilcox, *Anna the Prophetess*.

The Fourth Decade

The records indicate that it was the custom for the Secretary to send a greeting to each new Archbishop of York, to ask whether he was willing to continue the tradition of becoming Patron of the Society, and to invite him to come to Hull. But when Dr John S. Habgood became Primate in 1983, something apparently went wrong, though it is not clear whether it was an omission at this end or a secretarial lapse at Bishopthorpe Palace. At all events, in May 1987, the Archbishop was invited to make the customary Patronal visit and to deliver a lecture, and in his reply he wrote, 'I was indeed unaware that I was Patron of your Society – in fact I was unaware of its existence! But I am glad now to know about it, and feel that the least a Patron can do is to respond to your invitation.' He was as good as his word: on 7 December 1988 he gave a paper entitled, *Is all life intrinsically valuable?*

Closer links

The Agenda of the AGM for 5 May 1988 contains the first reference to the Department's annual Theology Day School, scheduled for 4 June 1988. The Society was, of course, *in* the University but not *of* it, prizing its independent 'Town and Gown' status, but there is no getting away from the fact that the University, through the Department of Theology, was its life-support machine, without which it could not have existed. At the same time, although one could not talk in terms of a symbiosis – the University could function without the Society, but not *vice versa* – there had undoubtedly been a measure of feed-back from the first. The Society, with its mixture of staff and 'outsiders', had been instrumental in bringing the most elite theological brains of the day on to the campus, and one example of the way in which this could be a two-way thing has already been recounted – the request to Eamon Duffy to address students on the morning after he had given his talk to the Society. And when, at the turn of the Millennium, the Department in its present form came under threat, no-one fought harder for it than the members of Hull and District Theological Society. Now, in the late 1980s, the two seemed to be coming even closer together, until it became almost as difficult to draw a distinct line between them as to separate a pair of Siamese twins.

Financially, the Society was not in a good position: speakers' expenses for the session had amounted to £59 and the coffee had cost £6.25, whereas subscriptions, including the 'individual lecture' charge, had brought in a total of £53.75. This had meant dipping into the reserves, leaving only £11.85 in the bank. So it was decided to raise the full subscription to £3, with £1 for students.

With their customary faith in the future, the committee had arranged an ambitious programme for the coming session, and, after this had been approved, Dr M. D. Goulder read a paper on *St John's Lent*.

* * * *

The threat of charges for room hire loomed over the AGM on 4 May 1989: 'In a general discussion of the Society's financial situation, it was reminded of impending changes in the University's room-booking policy and the prospect of having to pay hire charges,' read the minutes. 'Further, though no great increase was anticipated in speakers' expenses for 1989-90, it was assumed that in subsequent sessions there would be a considerable increase.'

It was agreed that the subscriptions should remain unchanged for the present, but that the committee should be empowered to raise them to £5, with £1 for students and 50p for individual meetings 'if further negotiations in the summer and autumn with the University warrant this'.

Mrs M. M. Flood, a long-serving member of the committee, retired with the thanks of the Society for her support, and the following officers were elected for 1989-1990: President, Mrs W. E. Sproston, Vice-President, Dr L. L. Grabbe, Secretary, Dr J. L. North, Treasurer, Mr F. Lyons. The committee comprised Mr D. Anderson, Miss A. Eccleston, Mrs J. Higginson, the Revd. Dr P. D. Stubley and the Revd. A. J. Wells. The draft programme for the following season was approved and it was announced that all future meetings would commence at 7.30 pm. Again, the Theology Day School was promoted, and after a paper read by Prof. J. Barr *The Literal, the Allegorical and Modern Biblical Scholarship,* the evening ended with discussion and a vote of thanks.

PROGRAMME 1987-1988

Friday, 18 October, 1987
> J. Wilton-Ely, Emeritus Professor of the History of Art, Hull University, *Architecture and Liturgy.*

Monday, 9 November
> Dr W. S. Campbell, Principal Lecturer in Religious Studies, Westhill College, Birmingham, *The Role of Paul in the Separation of early Christianity and Judaism.*

Thursday, 3 December
> Dr R.W. Ambler, Department of Adult and Continuing Education, Hull University, *Social Change and Religious Experience: Primitive Methodism in South Lincolnshire Society 1817-1875.*

Tuesday, 19 January, 1988
> Dr B. P. Thompson, Department of Theology, Hull University, *AIDS and the Churches*.

Monday, 15 February
> The Revd. Prof. J. W. Rogerson, Department of Biblical Studies, Sheffield University, *On Revising G. W. Anderson, 'The Living World of the Old Testament'*.

Tuesday, 8 March
> Students' Evening, speakers and titles to be announced.

Thursday, 5 May
> AGM. Dr M. D. Goulder, Department of Extramural Studies, Birmingham University, *St. John's Lent*.

Unless otherwise notified, all meetings are held in the Middleton Hall Meeting Room, basement floor, The Arts Building, Hull University, and commence at 7.45 pm.

The programme leaflet contains the following quotation: *'The worth of man does not consist in the truth he possesses, or thinks he possesses, but in the pains he has taken to attain that truth. For his powers are extended not through possession but through the search for truth. In this alone his ever-growing perfection consists. Possession makes him lazy, indolent and proud. If God held all truth in his right hand and in his left the everlasting striving after truth, so that I should always and everlastingly be mistaken, and said to me, 'Choose', with humility I would pick on the left hand and say, 'Father, grant me that. Absolute truth is for thee alone.'* G. E. Lessing.

PROGRAMME 1988-1989

Thursday, 27 October, 1988
> The Revd. G. A. Calvert, Chairman of the York and Hull Methodist District, *The Place of Methodism in the World Church*.

Monday, 14 November
> Prof. Erik C. Fudge, Professor Emeritus of Linguistics, Hull University, *Faith and Objectivity*.

Wednesday, 7 December
> Dr. J. S. Habgood, Archbishop of York, *Is all life instrinsically valuable?*

Thursday, 26 January, 1989
> Dr Joanna Weinberger, Lecturer in Rabbinics, Leo Baeck College, London, *The quest for Philo in sixteenth-century Jewish historiography*.

Monday, 6 February
> Dr Paul Ellingworth, United Bible Societies, *Translating the Bible: recent developments in theory and practice*.

Tuesday, 7 March
> Students' Evening. Mr Paul Cockman, The Revd. Karl Wray.

Thursday, 4 May
> AGM. The Revd. James Barr, Regius Professor of Hebrew, Oxford University. Title to be announced. *(The Literal, the Allegorical and Modern Biblical Scholarship).*
> Meetings held in the Middleton Hall Meeting Room.

Dispute

During the 1989-1990 season, the Society was innocently caught up in a *cause célèbre* which hit the national media and caused considerable embarrassment to the University.

To make some necessary cut-backs, certain members of staff were asked to accept early retirement or redundancy packages, and most agreed to do so, but Mr Edgar Page, a lecturer in the Department of Philosophy, declined, invoking a 'tenure' clause in his contract giving him the option of continuing in office up to the age of 67. The dispute escalated, one court supporting the University and another Mr Page. The affair finally reached the House of Lords, and one might say that it made legal history, resulting in the discontinuation of 'tenure' clauses in future contracts. The Unions backed Mr Page, and this caused action both on and off the campus, until an agreement between the parties was concluded.

At the Society's Annual General Meeting on 10 May 1990, 'It was agreed not to draw the attention of the University's officers to the fact that certain scholars invited to lecture to the Society during 1989-90 had declined the invitation in order to show solidarity with Mr Edgar Page.'

No doubt members felt that the University – their benefactor – was experiencing enough trouble over the affair, and they did not want to add to its problems.

A letter dated 12 December 1988 from John M. Hull, Reader in Religious Education at the University of Birmingham, to Secretary Lionel North, explains the situation:

'Dear Lionel North – Thank you for your letter of 29 November inviting me to visit the Hull and District Theological Society next autumn. I am afraid that a difficulty has arisen, and on 24 October I wrote to Dr. Farrell, the Pro-Chancellor of the University of Hull, withdrawing from my acceptance of the invitation to preach at the 1989 Service of Thanksgiving. I sent copies of my letter to the Registrar, the Guild of Students and leading Church people in the Hull area.

'The reason for my withdrawal is that the Association of University Teachers, of which I am a member, is in dispute with the University of Hull over the dismissal of Mr Edgar Page from the Department of Philosophy. This is the first such dismissal to have taken place in any university in this country and has been greeted with widespread dismay by university academics. The policy of the AUT is that we should break off all association and support extended to the University until this dispute is settled.

'That means that I will not now be coming to Hull on the date in question. No doubt the University will obtain another preacher and it would probably be best if you asked that person to visit the Theological Society.

'I am sure you will understand with what mixed feelings I am writing this letter. On the one hand, I am conscious of the honour of being asked, and regret very much not being able to accept. At the same time I am sure you will appreciate my sense of obligation to the AUT and how wrong it would be for me to come to Hull in the present circumstances.'

* * * *

It is recorded that 'fourteen members and friends of the Society were in attendance at the meeting'. Annual meetings are not popular even when there are important or contentious matters to discuss, and a first-class speaker into the bargain

The Treasurer's report drew attention to 'the healthiest credit balance since 1982'* But, to prevent complacency, he added that the figures implied a membership strength seven less than in the previous year. It was agreed to keep the existing subscription rates 'if the Society was not billed by the University during the summer for room hire'. If it were, the officers had power to raise full membership to £5. 'In any case there was every likelihood that such a rise would be sought at the next AGM with effect from October 1991.' The Secretary introduced a discussion on the poor attendances at some of the Society's meetings over the previous three years, and sought advice on how to tackle this. Names of useful contacts were tendered.

The list of officers and committee remained unchanged, and the programme proposed for 1990-1991 was accepted. Sara Dodd presented an illustrated lecture, *Holman Hunt and the High Church* – and generously provided the coffee to accompany the closing discussion!

*It is not how clear he calculates this. The recorded figures are: 1982, £23.09; 1983, £42.17; 1984, £41.90; 1985, £53.82; 1986 (missing); 1987, £22.69; 1988, £11.85; 1989, £30.13; 1990, £57.81 – a veritable seesaw, depending largely on the expenses of visiting speakers.

* * * *

After the touch of drama which marked the 1990 AGM, the neatly handwritten minutes of the meeting on 8 May 1991 come as something of an anticlimax, though they did contain good news: membership was up by 13 over the previous year, and for the first time the credit balance was in three figures, £124.18. It was agreed to maintain the current subscription rates for the coming year.

The resignation of Mrs Wendy Sproston from the Presidency was accepted with regret, and she was thanked for her years of service to the

Society. Her place was taken by Dr L. L. Grabbe, and the other officers were re-elected, along with the committee.

A plug for the Department's Theology Day School had now become routine, and, after the draft programme for 1991-1992 had been approved, Dr Keith Elliott read a paper entitled, *Sayings of Jesus Outside the Gospels.*

* * * *

By the date of the 1992 AGM, 6 May, the threat of room charges had still not materialised, and, with a healthy £121.61 in the bank, it was proposed that the student fee should be dropped.

However, one member, Mr Hodgson, drew attention to the fact that there was a shortfall of £50 and that the Society was living on its balances. He suggested that the student fee should stand, but be waived, and this compromise was accepted.

Officers and committee were returned for a further year, and, after the usual formalities, Dr Peter Sedgwick delivered a paper on *Theology, Nationalism and Europe,* which was followed by 'a lively discussion'.

PROGRAMME 1989-1990

Wednesday, 18 October, 1989
  Mr John Biggs, Department of Chemistry, Hull University, President of the Baptist Union of Gt. Britain and Ireland, 1989-1990, *Our Stewardship of Creation.*

Thursday, 9 November
  The Revd. Andrew Louth, Principal Lecturer in Religious Studies, Goldsmith's College, London, *Reflections on the Idea of Creation in the Early Church.*

Wednesday, 6 December
  Dr T. T. B. Ryder, Department of Classics, Hull University, *Dwellers in Phrygia and Pamphilia as seen by a stranger from Britain April 1989,* (with slides).

Wednesday, 24 January, 1990
  Dr Peter Forster, Department of Sociology and Social Anthropology, Hull University, *Christian Missions and 'African Tradition'.*

Monday, 19 February
  Students' Evening, titles to be announced.

Monday, 12 March
  Dr John C. Davies, Department of English, Bishop Grosseteste College, Lincoln, *Narrative and the Terror of History.*

Thursday, 10 May
  AGM. Ms Sara Dodd, Department of History, Hull University, *Holman Hunt and the High Church* (with slides).
  Meetings held in the Education Block on the South Side of the Library, at 7.30 pm.

The programme leaflet also advertised some of the meetings of a 'sister organisation', the Humberside Association for Religious and Moral Education, held in The Avenue Centre, Park Avenue, Hull:

13 November, 1989
    Dr Kim Knott, Department of Theology and Religious Studies, Leeds University, *Hinduism in Leeds*.

22 January, 1990
    Jean Harrison, Secondary Education Adviser for Christian Aid, *Christian Aid in Schools*.

5 March
    Michael Wardlow, HMI, *RE Provided?* (Meeting at Baysgarth School, Barton, S. Humberside).

2 April
    Dr John Hall, Faculty of Education, Birmingham University, *Compulsory Worship – a contradiction in terms*.

21 May
    Dr Graham Miles, Lecturer in Religious Studies, Homerton College, Cambridge, *Understanding Religious Experience in the Classroom*.

18 June
    Visit to Hindu Temple in Bradford.
    (Contact for further information, Lorna Caygill, Hull 632543).

PROGRAMME 1990-1991

Thursday, 1 November, 1990
    Dr Valerie Sanders, Department of English, Buckingham University, *Religion and the Victorian Woman*.

Monday, 19 November
    Mr Clive Lawton, Headmaster, King David High School, Liverpool, *Concepts of the Messiah*.

Thursday, 6 December
    Canon Dr John Atherton, Manchester Cathedral, *Market Economics: the challenge to Christian thought*.

Friday, 25 January, 1991
    The advertised speaker was Mr John James USPG, Pune, India. *Making Indian Christianity more Indian – first impressions* (with slides). But due to his indisposition the paper on this occasion was given by the new Lecturer in Historical Theology at Hull, Dr David Bagchi. His paper was entitled *Did he fall or was he pushed? Luther's theological development and his Catholic literary opponents, 1518-1521*.

Thursday, 5 February
    Canon Dr Francis Gordon-Kerr, Vicar of Welton with Melton, and Rural Dean of Hull, *The Consequences of Training for Ministry in the Church*.

Wednesay, 6 March
> The Revd. Gerhard Becker, Pastor, German Lutheran Church, Hull, *The Protestant Churches in Contemporary Germany.*

Wednesday, 8 May
> AGM. Dr J. Keith Elliott, Department of Theology and Religious Studies Leeds University, *Sayings of Jesus Outside the Gospels: Problems of Canon and Text.*

> Meetings held in the Education Block on the South Side of the Library.

> The Theology Day School will be held in the University on Saturday, 8 June, beginning at 10 am. The speakers are Dr Haddon Wilmer, University of Leeds, and Dr Peter Sedgwick, University of Hull. Their theme is *Salvation in Christ.* For further information, contact the Department of Adult and Continuing Education.

PROGRAMME 1991-1992

Thursday, 31 October, 1991
> Prof. Adrian Hastings, Department of Theology and Religious Studies, Leeds University, *Reflections on problems involved in writing 'Robert Runcie' in the light of its reviews.*

Monday, 18 November
> The Revd. Prof. A. G. Dyson, Faculty of Theology, Manchester University, *Anglican Respectability and Social Theology: the case of Hastings Rashdall.*

Tuesday, 10 December
> Dr David Parker, Queen's College, Birmingham (Title to be announced).

Wednesday, 22 January, 1992
> Dr Michael Wintle, Department of Dutch Studies, Hull University, *Papists, Pillars and Protestants: Theology and Religion in the Netherlands since 1800.*

Tuesday, 18 February
> Mrs June Higginson, Hull University, *Chronology in John: Fact or Fiction.*

Monday, 9 March
> The Revd. Dr David Jasper, Faculty of Theology, Glasgow University, *The Study of Literature and Theology: where do we go from here?*

Wednesday, 6 May
> AGM. Dr Peter Sedgwick, Hull University (Title in programme, *Theology and Society in the United States.* Paper delivered, *Theology, Nationalism and Europe).*

> Meetings held in the Education Centre.

> The Theology Day School will be held in the University on Saturday, 6 June 1992, beginning at 10 am. The theme is *The Catholicity of the Protestant Reformation.*

All Change!

Elections at the AGM on 18 May 1993 saw several changes: Dr L. L. Grabbe resigned from the Presidency and was replaced by Dr Lionel North, whose office as Secretary was taken over by the Revd. Dr Peter Stubley. The Revd. Adrian Wells also left the committee.

As the Treasurer, Frank Lyons, was unable to be present, there was no discussion about subscription rates, but cash in the bank registered a satisfactory £121.61, and speakers' expenses for the year had amounted to just £17.00.

Speaker of the evening was Prof. Norman Whybray, making a welcome return visit to Hull, his subject, *The Wisdom Psalms*. 'The paper provoked a good response and a very lively discussion,' the minutes record.

* * * *

The manner in which Town and Gown were drawing ever closer together in matters theological is apparent from the minutes of the AGM on 10 May 1994, held in Lecture Theatre D in the Larkin Building.

President Lionel North spoke about the coming Day School on 11 June and said that he hoped members would broadcast the event among their acquaintances. Dr Elfride Bickersteth requested that the Adult Education Department be informed about the days of special Orthodox Devotion, so that future Day Schools would not clash with one of these services, as had happened that year. This would enable Dr Hillary Carby-Hall to attend the Day School.

Dr North drew the attention of the assembly – numbering nine members and two guests – to the dwindling number of members, and posed a question about the level at which the subjects for discussion were pitched: 'Members assented that the level of subjects was soundly pitched. However, it was noted that, when a popular and well-known person was the speaker, the attendance was always very good.'

Membership levels and finance inevitably go together, and the Treasurer's report was followed by a discussion on a proposed increase of 66.6% in the fee for full membership (£3.00 to £5.00) and 50% for students (£1 to £1.50), but written alterations on the file copy of the minutes indicate that the final decision was to leave the student fee as it was, and to load the increase on to the single-meeting charge, making it £1.00. Cash in the bank was £68.63. Officers were re-elected for a further year, and at the presentation of the 1994-1995 programme, Dr Bickersteth suggested that the Society's Patron, the Archbishop of York, might be invited to speak on 'a science-related subject'.

Business concluded, Mr John G. Bernasconi gave an illustrated paper, *Religious Art and the Spectator in the Italian Renaissance*. 'The paper was very informative, greatly welcomed and appreciated by all present' was the verdict, and the President proposed a special vote of thanks 'in consideration of the speaker, who had foregone a place at High Table in order to give his lecture'!

The Society's files also contain a notice of a Postgraduate Research seminar run by the Department of Theology in the Education Centre in the Spring Term of 1994: Friday, 25 February, the Revd. Alan Payne, of Leeds, *The Quality of Humanity.*

Friday, 18 March, Dr Elaine Graham of Manchester University, *Making a Difference: Towards a Theology of Gender.* Contact, the Revd. Peter Sedgwick.

PROGRAMME 1992-1993

Tuesday, 20 October, 1992
  Dr L. Ritmeyer, Manchester University, *The Temple Mount in the time of Jesus* (with slides)
Thursday, 26 November
  Canon John Atherton, Manchester Cathedral, *Christian Responses to the Social Market Economy.*
Wednesday, 9 December
  Mr Louis Billington, Hull University, *Popular Evangelicalism in England, Scotland and North America 1740-1840.*
Thursday, 21 January, 1993
  Mr S.A. J. Bradley, York University, *Images of the Godhead in Anglo-Saxon Literature and Art* (with slides).
Wednesday, 17 February
  Prof. Robert C. Walton, University of Münster im W., Germany, *The Swiss Reformation and Marsilio of Padua.*
Monday, 8 March
  Prof. David B. Pearson, Hull University, *Birth, Death and the Universe: the new cosmology and faith.*
Wednesday, 11 May
  AGM. Emeritus Prof. R Norman Whybray, Ely, *The Wisdom Psalms.*

Meetings held in the Education Centre.

The Theology Day School will be held in the University on Saturday, 5 June 1993, beginning at 10 am. The theme is *Christology and the Gospels.*

PROGRAMME 1993-1994

Monday, 25 October, 1993
  Dr John F. Healey, Department of Middle Eastern Studies, Manchester University, *The Pagan God: Middle Eastern Religions in the New Testament Period.* (with slides)
Thursday, 11 November
  Dr Haddon Wilmer, Department of Theology and Religious Studies, Leeds University, *God and the Unforgivable in Politics.*

Tuesday, 18 January, 1994
: Mr Geoff Caygill, Friends of Israel Association (Hull and District), *The Kibbutz* (with slides).

Tuesday, 15 February
: Dr Ann Loades, Department of Theology, Durham University, *Dorothy Sayers on Dante, Love and Freedom*.

Thursday, 17 March
: Dr Clyde Binfield, Department of History, Sheffield University, *'A Crucible of Modest though Concentrated Experiment': Some Reflections on Church and People in an Industrial City*.

Tuesday, 10 May
: AGM. Mr John G. Bernasconi, Department of History, Hull University, *Religious Art and the Spectator in the Italian Renaissance*.

Meetings held in the Larkin Building.

The Theology Day School will he held in the University on Saturday, 11 June, 1994, beginning at 10 am. The theme will be taken from Old Testament Studies.

Growing concern

It was not lack of funds which caused concern at the AGM on 9 May 1995 – there was £122.58 in the bank, and no travelling expenses had been incurred for the majority of the speakers – but dwindling membership. Only 10 members and one guest attended the meeting, and the Secretary, Peter Stubley, suggested that perhaps May was not the best time to hold it, due to the long break between the end of the Spring Term and the beginning of the Summer Term. The reorganisation of the academic year was affecting many aspects of university life for both staff and students, and the President, Dr Lionel North, proposed that members should defer any decision on an alternative date until the effects of the change from three terms to two semesters had been assessed. Dr Elfride Bickersteth suggested that the meeting could continue to be held in May but take place before an annual dinner.

The Treasurer, Frank Lyons, set each member a challenge to recruit a new member before the new session in October: 'The present paid-up membership has averaged 21 for the past eight years, compared with 43 in 1984,' he reported. 'Only by returning to the 1984 level of membership can the Society maintain a sound financial basis.' It was decided to maintain the student subscription at £1.00. The committee were re-elected *en bloc*, and the 1995-1996 programme was discussed and approved.

Prof. David Palliser read a paper entitled, *The Reformation: Babies and Bathwater?* concentrating on the Reformation in England at the social level, drawing together evidence from wills which illustrated that for many provincial citizens of importance the Reformation had been gradual. The paper provoked a divergence of questions and an informative discussion, 'greatly appreciated by all present'.

PROGRAMME 1994-1995

Thursday, 20 October, 1994
  Prof. James Dunn, Department of Theology, Durham University, *Was Paul Converted?*

Monday, 14 November
  Dr Susan Parsons, Principal, East Midlands Ministry Course, *The Theological and Ethical Challenge of Post Modernism.*

Wednesday, 7 December
  The Revd. Rod Garner, East Riding Training Team, *The Love of God and the World's Pain.*

Tuesday, 17 January, 1995
  Dr Stephen Carr, Hull University, *Cutting the Apron Strings: Theology and Parental Images.*

Tuesday, 28 February
  The Most Revd. Dr John Habgood, Archbishop of York, *The Search for a Christian Social Ethic.*

Thursday, 16 March
  The Revd. Jim Poore, Beverley, *Realism and Non-Realism in Theology.*

Tuesday, 9 May
  AGM. Prof David Palliser, Leeds University, *The Reformation: Babies and Bathwater?*

Meetings held in the Education Centre.

The Theology Day School will he held in the University on Saturday, 10 June 1995, beginning at 10 am. Theme: *Study of World Religions.*

Importunate?

Persuading distinguished speakers to address the Society sometimes required consummate diplomacy and persistence. Letters exchanged between Secretary Peter Stubley and Dr Carol Harrison, who had met briefly during their earlier university life, read almost like a delicate courtship, worthy of the pen of Jane Austen. Replying to Peter Stubley's invitation to read a paper to the Society, Dr Harrison wrote, 'I'm sorry I can't say yes to giving a paper to the Society, but feel honoured to be asked. The problem is my two-year-old son, who will not sleep if I'm not there to put him to bed! He may have changed by the end of the year, but I don't like to leave him.'

Not to be discouraged, the Secretary tried again on 7 December 1994: 'I hope I am not importunate in writing again to ask if you could come to read a paper to our Society during our next season, if your domestic circumstances allow.' And, to gild the lily, he continued, 'What about May 1996? The nights are light, and we may be able to offer you a lift to York Railway Station so that you could be home that night.' Who could resist such blandishments? 'Yes, you are importunate,' replied the lady, 'but yes, I'll come.' And come she did, on 14 May 1996, to speak on *The Silent Majority:*

the Fathers' Attitude to the Family – a domestic-sounding title, but the word 'Fathers" is plural and has a capital 'F', which suggests a Patristic theme!

* * * *

The End?

Crisis-point came in the spring of 1996. On 28 April, President Lionel North sent a letter to members of the committee in which he said, 'I think that our business meeting this year must consider something that I don't think we have had to face before. We have all been aware for several years of a declining membership, and the fact that on his retirement Peter Stubley will resign his secretaryship at this AGM, and that we may have difficulty in finding a suitable replacement only makes that decline more obvious. Peter has prepared the programme for '96-'97, but, if we do not find a new secretary, and if membership does not pick up, we must face up to the possibility of closing the Society at the AGM in May 1997. We cannot continue to expect speakers to travel considerable distances for only travelling expenses, to address a small audience. I find this more and more embarrassing.' Dr North asked the committee for their views, and stated his intention to put these matters on the agenda for the Annual General Meeting on 14 May 1996.

* * * *

The AGM opened with a cheerful report from Treasurer Frank Lyons. The £5 full membership subscription had helped to raise the bank balance to £151.09. But there was a paid-up membership of only 18.

Dr North repeated the substance of his letter to the committee, and proposed that if there were no increase in numbers (at the previous five meetings the attendance had fluctuated between 10 and 15) the Society should close at the end of 1997: 'Our "regulars" do not include any younger people who could be regarded as the nucleus for the future.'

The 1996-1997 programme was already prepared and the bank balance 'favourable'. 'But it is embarrassing to invite speakers and then have so few members.'

Discussion followed. It was not thought helpful to contact presbyteries with details of the programme, and the practicality of arranging a programme for 1997-1998 presented problems. But Dr Carol Harrison, the evening's speaker, suggested that speakers with a continuity of subject, or whose subject tied in with undergraduate studies, might be helpful ('cf. the Durham experience'). There were suggestions of a dinner, a public debate or 'a meeting over a drink'. Dr North called for further suggestions to be put forward over the summer, and proposed that the committee should continue in office, to which the meeting assented. Peter Stubley was thanked for arranging the programme and for his work as Secretary over the previous three years.

Anticipating Dr John Habgood's retirement as Archbishop of York it was agreed that the Society should acknowledge his past patronage and should welcome his successor, Dr David Hope. The evening concluded with Dr Carol Harrison's talk,

PROGRAMME 1995-1996

Monday, 16 October,1995
> The Revd. Malcolm Brown, William Temple Foundation, Manchester, *It's the Economy, Stupid'*: Fragmentation, Globalisation and Mission.* *A quote from US. President Bill Clinton's election campaign.

Monday, 6 November
> Dr Edward Abramson, Department of American Studies, Hull University, *Job: Jew or Christian?* (In place of the advertised speaker, the Revd. Dr William Telford, whose talk was postponed owing to the illness of his wife).

Thursday, 14 December
> Dr Alistair McFadyen, Leeds University, *Sexual Abuse of Children and the Doctrine of Sin.*

Wednesday, 24 January, 1996
> Dr Elaine Graham, Manchester University, *Practising Communities: Pastoral Theology, Pluralism and Post-Modernism.*

Tuesday, 20 February
> Dr John Bradshaw, former Director of Hull City Museums and Art Galleries, *Religious Paintings by the Pre-Raphaelites.*

Wednesday, 6 March
> Dr David Bagchi, Hull University, *Defender of the Faith or Defender of Faiths? The future of a royal title.*

Tuesday, 14 May
> AGM. Dr Carol Harrison, Durham University, *The Silent Majority: the Fathers' Attitude to the Family.*

> The Theology Day School will be held in the University on Saturday, 8 June, 1996, beginning at 10.00 am. Theme: *New Testament Studies.* The main speaker will be Prof Morna Hooker of Cambridge University

PROGRAMME 1996-1997

Wednesday, 23 October, 1996
> The Revd. Peter Sedgwick, Assistant Secretary, B.S.R., *Towards an Urban Theology.*

Thursday, 7 November
> The Revd. Dr William Telford, Newcastle University, *Is the New Testament Antisemitic?*

Monday, 16 December
> Prof. Brian Moloney, Hull University, *St Francis of Assisi and the Canticle of the Creatures.*

Tuesday, 21 January, 1997
> The Revd. Peter Stubley, Hon. Fellow in the School of Humanities, Department of Theology, Hull University, *Christians and the Modern World: A Secular Spirituality.*

Tuesday, 18 February
> The Revd. Canon Dr John Toy, Chancellor, York Minster, *What is Genesis about? Choosing sixteen scenes for the new Great West Door of York Minster.*

Tuesday, 18 March
> The Revd. Dr Elizabeth Culling, Chaplain, Bishop Burton College, Senior Adviser in Rural Affairs to the Archbishop of York, Priest in Charge, Cherry Burton, *Is there such a thing as Celtic Spirituality?*

Monday, 12 May
> AGM. Dr Peter Large, Department of Biological Sciences, Hull University, *The Old Catholic Church, its History and Modern Developments.*

Meetings held in Lecture Theatre E in the Larkin Building.

The Theology Day School will be held in the University on Saturday, 7 June, 1997, beginning at 10 am. The theme will be taken from Reformation Studies.

* * * *

Judging by the range and quality of this programme, it is clear that, if the Society was about to close, it was certainly going to go out with a bang!

In fact, a new era was just about to begin.

The Fifth Decade

The Society suspended its activities after the Annual General Meeting on 12 May 1997, when the committee resigned. The main problem identified by the outgoing committee was the steady decline in the numbers attending meetings, which made it impossible for them to continue. It had become unreasonable to expect distinguished speakers to address such small audiences.

Various ways of improving attendance were examined, from the relatively straightforward to the radical, but the majority of those present at the AGM were against winding up the Society altogether. A 'holding committee' consisting of Dr David Bagchi as acting-President and the Revd. Dr Michael Wilson as acting-Secretary, was elected on the understanding that they would re--launch the Society at a later date.

At the Theology Department's Day School on 7 June 1997, Dr Wilson circulated a questionnaire inviting comments about the sort of Society the respondents would like to see emerge. He received some 20 returns in all – an encouragingly high response in the circumstances. Many chose to add comments and suggestions, and these are reproduced below;

* * * *

Summary of responses to Michael Wilson's questionnaire
of 7 June 1997

'I myself was satisfied with the Society up till now, both in content and in style. It should continue to concern itself with religious matters in an objective way that is acceptable to those of no fixed belief as well as to adherents of a specific faith. Speakers should never therefore assume that those present all share Christian presuppositions. But the new Society should meet in a user-friendly atmosphere (i.e. not in a big, formal lecture theatre) and should provide time and facilities for chat over tea and coffee as it always used to do in the 1970s.'

'I like listening to lectures from which I can learn something, so I should be sorry if the Society simply became a discussion group. I think that there must be people who would like to belong but who have not heard about it, so what it needs is a good advertising campaign, with an attractive leaflet widely distributed.'

'A place for discussion and airing of views by members. Input by the informed – including professionals. Time: a half-session in daytime

(Saturday morning for preference), 4 times a year.'

'[Should be] varied: lectures and discussions, contributions from members, etc. Time: Saturday half-session [and/or] weekday evenings.'

'1) Conversation time; 2) local speakers (to save expense)? 3) annual event – lunch or dinner?; 4) evenings preferred.'

'Two Saturday Theology Days per year – as today. Two other gatherings per year – maybe evenings to suit a few more people.'

'Lectures and discussions. Would an occasional Any Questions forum be possible?'

'Lectures and discussions.'

'My particular interest is in the application of theology to contemporary society. Speakers/events which help to illuminate the relevance of theology to aspects of contemporary society, e.g. the market economy, globalisation, unemployment etc. are particularly helpful. A more contributory format would sometimes be attractive. My preferred time would be a weekday, either lunch-time or evening.'

'Emphasis on Biblical and historical studies (as study days of 1996, 1997), or series of 4 weekly meetings on topics above – Saturdays?'

'I enjoyed the previous format. Would wish for intellectual stimulation. I enjoy topics with which I am unfamiliar as well as those with which I am familiar – need my brain "stretching". Would not wish for church-type biblical study.'

'1) 3/4 meetings a year – at least; 2) topics pre-advertised – time for research – perhaps even mailing out notes prior to talks; 3) could meet in homes – more social – supper – coffee.'

'Events for the current Theological Society have not been publicised enough. Guest speakers are the obvious request, but a little more frequent would be desirable. If this were not possible then more frequent events involving Hull theologians would still be desirable, and I'm sure popular. Small group discussion may allow more questions to be posed, and also reduce the fear of not appearing academically uninformed (informed?).'

'It might be that a mixed format may provide a better arrangement giving chance for informal sharing and introduction of new thoughts, etc.'

Principles and Proposals

From these responses and from the events which had brought the Society to this point some general principles were deduced and practical proposals put forward for the future direction of the Society.

First, the stark question had to be asked and debated: was Hull and District Theological Society an idea whose time had passed? The loyal membership was ageing; its programmes, however starry and well-advertised, could not be expected to compete with people's increasingly busy professional, social and domestic lives. This seemed to be the analysis of the outgoing committee, and the small band of enthusiasts seeking to preserve the institution had to accept the force of much of it.

On the other hand, it would in their eyes be a shame if England's twelfth city were unable to sustain a society of this sort. There were no signs of any dwindling of interest in theology elsewhere in the country – even Cambridge physicists were having to mention God if they wanted their books to sell! But there were alternative and complementary ways of 'doing theology', such as that offered by the Institute of Community Theology recently established in York, and perhaps these could be considered.

The stated purpose of the Society – 'The study of theology in all its branches' – implied both depth and breadth of intellectual engagement, and it was agreed that there should be no 'dumbing down' of the meetings, which should continue to be attractive to everyone in the region with an intelligent interest in theology. This was not, however, incompatible with the aim of making the meetings more open, welcoming and friendly.

The 'semi-detached' relationship between Society and University was seen as an advantage, because, in theory at least, it meant that the Society could function as Hull's premier forum for theological debate and the circulation of ideas for both town and gown.

It followed from that premise that the Society needed to work much more closely with the appropriate bodies in the region whose business was, or included, theology – churches, training courses and RE departments of schools and colleges.

To achieve this, improved publicity was vital. Past programmes had been extremely good, but poorly publicised, even within the University, so the production and distribution of the term card, and additional posters and handbills if funds permitted, was to be considered the first call on resources The Society had been very good in the past at getting term cards to local clergy, but not so good at reaching their congregations, and help needed to be sought in the distribution of material, together with ideas for potential targets.

Alternative venues for meetings were also considered both on and off the University campus, with preference for those in which refreshments could be served before or after the talk.

Ambitious ideas

The proposals drawn up by acting-President David Bagchi for the new-look Society's 1998-1999 programme might appear decidedly over-ambitious, having regard to the parlous situation at the time, but it is amazing how many of them were actually implemented in that period, while others provided ideas and aspirations for future action.

A full programme of seven meetings was proposed, with an experimental Saturday session in early May 1999, along the lines of the Theology Department's annual Day School, which could be combined with the AGM.

The notion of an 'Any Questions' evening also found favour – after all, it was known that theology faculties used to hold them regularly in the Middle Ages! Another suggestion was an event of special interest to local Sixth Formers taking Religious Studies at A-level – something on the lines of *The Jesus of History v the Christ of Faith*, or on bioethics. A debate involving two speakers, and a themed programme for the whole season on a subject such as 'Current Issues in Theology', with sessions on 'Theological Education', 'Historical Theology', 'Theology and Spirituality', 'New Testament Theology', 'Philosophical Theology' and 'Bioethics', plus an evening devoted to papers given by graduate students, were also on the list. So there was no shortage of constructive concepts when plans were made for the re-launching of the Society in the autumn of 1998.

Revived

During the rest of 1998, the Society remained suspended but by no means inactive. The funds were tapped to pay the expenses of Dr Loveday Alexander, who gave a lecture on *The Role of the Book in the Early Church* under the auspices of the Society and the Department of Theology on 18 May 1998. And behind the scenes much discussion and planning was taking place with a view to producing a themed programme of meetings on the lines suggested by the acting-President.

What had emerged from conversations between members, and was confirmed in the responses to the questionnaire, was the importance of restoring a social element to the meetings. If there were some who would have preferred to listen to a lecture undistracted, they were in the minority; for most, the chance to mingle and talk over a cup of coffee – even if the brew was not of the finest quality – was vital, otherwise one might as well stay at home and read a book! In the early meetings of the revived Society, there was much portering of kettles and teapots, packets of biscuits and slices of cake, until arrangements were made with the University's catering service to provide the essentials, to be enhanced with a few extra dainties on special occasions such as the Christmas meeting, when wine glasses replaced the tea and coffee cups.

The re-launch of the Society in the Graduate Research Centre on Wednesday, 21 October 1998, was therefore celebrated with a reception in the Common Room before a lecture given in the Semester Room by the Revd. Jim Jones, Director of the Institute for Community Theology and Religious Heritage, York, on *Community Theology*.

Plans made

On Wednesday, 2 December 1998, an Extraordinary General Meeting was held in the same venue. There were no minutes of the 1997 AGM, but Dr Bagchi outlined the salient events of that meeting, and these corresponded with the recollections of those who had been present.

He then introduced a paper, which had previously been circulated, based on the 1957 Rules of the Society, suggesting that this might be used as the basis of a revised Constitution. Any formal change would have to be left to the 1999 AGM, but comments were invited on the draft as it stood. It was welcomed in general terms, with minor alteration, and the meeting agreed that it should be presented at the next Annual General Meeting.

No nominations had been received for new officers and committee, but Mrs Barbara Robinson was nominated and seconded from the floor, and provisionally elected as an Ordinary Member. Elections for the remaining vacancies were held over until the AGM, and it was agreed that Dr Bagchi should continue as acting-President until then.

The Society's account stood at £47.98, following the withdrawal of funds to pay for Dr Alexander's lecture. It was reported that Dr Wilson's questionnaire had revealed that some members were prepared to pay considerably more than the current £5 subscription if this could help to secure speakers from outside the immediate area. After some discussion, it was decided to raise the annual rate for full membership to £10.00 and the charge for attendance at individual meetings by non-members (other than as a guest of a member) to £2.00 per meeting. Students in full-time education would be allowed to join free of charge.

At the close of business, Dr Adrian Worsfold, Research Student in Hull University's Department of Theology, read a paper on *The Hull Unitarian Church: historical and sociological perspectives,* so continuing the Society's tradition of concluding each General Meeting with an interesting and informative talk.

* * * *

Continuing the lecture-programme: On Tuesday, 2 February 1999, the Rt. Revd. Dr. David Tustin, Bishop of Grimsby, spoke on *The Development of Anglican-Lutheran relations in the twentieth century;* and on Wednesday, 17 March, the Revd. Dr Michael Wilson, Methodist Minister at Hessle, spoke on *Philosophical Theology.*

The highlight of the year, however, came on Saturday, 1 May 1999, with a presentation by Dr June Boyce-Tillman, of King Alfred's College, Winchester, entitled *Hildegard of Bingen: theology and mysticism.* Held in the tranquil setting of the University Chapel, the event commemorated the 900th anniversary of the birth of the 12th-century abbess, a revival of whose music had recently made the top selection in the popular charts.

Dr Boyce-Tillman evoked the spirit of the mystic nun through poetry, painting, vocal and instrumental music – and even inspired the audience to attempt a medieval version of line-dancing!

The meeting was well-attended, and undoubtedly helped to rebuild the image of the Society as a body which successfully blended tradition with innovation. To many of those present it seemed like a turning-point.

* * * *

The presentation was followed by the Annual General Meeting at which decisions made at the EGM on 2 December were ratified and adopted.

Dr Bagchi opened the proceedings by proposing a vote of thanks to Dr Lionel North and Dr Wendy Sproston North, who were to retire at the end of the academic year and move to Darlington. He reminded the meeting of the many years of service they had rendered to the Society, both as members and as officers, and he attributed the fact that the Society had continued to thrive into its 42nd year in no small part to their tireless and much appreciated work.

'They will be remembered among other things for their success in charming, cajoling and coercing a wide range of interesting speakers to make the journey to Hull, including most of the leading names of theological, and especially Biblical, scholarship in this country,' he said. 'They will also be remembered for their ability to put the most apprehensive of speakers at their ease.'

The meeting unanimously endorsed these words and, following the meeting, the new committee elected the 'Doctors North' honorary members, 'in recognition of their exceptional service to the Society', and wished them a long and happy retirement.

The draft Constitution was discussed and adopted, with some minor amendments.

The provisional programme for 1999-2000 was then discussed. Preference was expressed for a Saturday daytime meeting in May (but avoiding Bank Holiday weekends) since the 1999 experiment had proved so successful.

It was thought that something of interest to sixth-form tutors and their pupils, related to the A-Level Religious Studies syllabus, might be very useful, especially if the speaker were a name known to the pupils from text-books and the like, though it was recognised that a meeting so late in the year would benefit only pupils in the lower-sixth. The Revd. Rodney Ward recommended for this purpose Dr Peter Vardy, who had given the 1998 Chaplaincy Lecture at the University of Lincolnshire and Humberside.

As no nominations had been received for officers and Ordinary Committee Members, Dr Bagchi invited nominations from the floor, with the following results:

President, Dr David Bagchi, nominated by the Revd. Stephen Deas, seconded by Dr Elfride Bickersteth.

Hon. Secretary, Mrs Barbara Robinson, nominated by Mrs Linda Richards, seconded by Mrs Mary Rose Kearney.

Hon. Treasurer, Mrs Linda Richards, nominated by Mrs Mary Rose Kearney, seconded by the Revd. Stephen Deas.

Ordinary Members, the Revd. Stephen Deas, Mrs Mary Rose Kearney, the Revd. Rodney Ward.

There being no other nominations, Dr Bagchi declared all those nominated duly elected, and thanked both nominees and proposers for their enthusiasm. It was noted that a vacancy still existed for an Ordinary Member.

Reporting on the financial situation, the newly-elected President said that no balance of accounts had been presented because, in the absence of a Treasurer, payments could be made only into the Society's account. Cheques could not be written, so no 'balance' for the year existed. The account, however, stood at £198.27 at 28 April 1999. This was owed partly to the generosity of the Department of Theology, which had subsidised mailings to members, partly to the Graduate Research Centre, which had allowed the Society to hold its evening meetings free of rent or porterage charges, and partly to the generosity of the year's speakers, only two of whom had asked for their travel expenses.

Membership now stood at 17 Full Members and one Student Member, compared with the figures in May 1996 – 16 Full Members and no Student Members.

Mary Rose Kearney raised the question of publicity, pointing out that the Society's programme had not been advertised in her church, and that she had had to copy her own programme for those interested.

The President replied that he had taken four publicity initiatives over the year. The first was to publicise the programme through the KEY Churches' Newsletter, which was posted directly to church secretaries in the HU postal area, rather than through incumbents. The second was to issue four mailings to Society members instead of the usual one. The third was to advertise the talks in the University Bulletin. And the fourth was to make posters/flyers for display in the Arts Faculty and for distribution to members. However, he recognised that these steps alone were inadequate, and that it was necessary to reach new audiences.

Rodney Ward suggested that the Hull Inter-Faith Forum might be interested in receiving the programmes; Mary Rose Kearney suggested trying the publication *What's on in Hull?;* and Stephen Deas offered to advertise the meetings of the Society at chapter meetings of the Hull Deanery clergy.

Elfride Bickersteth reminded members that the Society was for everyone in the area who had an intelligent interest in theology, not just for believers or church-goers, and that the publicity strategy should reflect that, while Linda Richards urged that the Society should develop its social side and put on at least one dinner a year. She offered to explore publicity opportunities on the Society's behalf.

Winding up the business of the meeting, the President thanked the members for their support over the previous year. Attendances had been very healthy compared with those which had led to the resignation of the last committee in 1997, and they had entirely justified the efforts of those who had worked to revive the Society. In particular, he referred to the Rev. Dr. Michael Wilson, who had done sterling work, 'especially in master-minding the questionnaire which threw up many good and interesting ideas including the idea of a Saturday meeting'. With the establishment of a dynamic new committee and an intriguing programme of talks for 1999-2000, the President had every confidence that next May he would be able to report on the conclusion of an even more successful year.

Revision

Much of the Constitution remained unchanged in the subsequent revision, proving that the original Rules had served the Society well for 40 years, and that the basic principles on which it was founded were still valid. But times had changed, and some up-dating was obviously needed, including the simplification of the title to: 'The name of the Society shall be The Hull and District Theological Society.'

Gender-inclusiveness, long taken for granted, now had to be explicit ('he or she'). National Service had ended (to the regret of many disciplinarians!) and Rule 4b now read, 'Unwaged persons and those studying full-time at a recognised school, college or university may be allowed to become members without charge.' The full annual subscription was amended to the agreed £10.

It had been the recent practice of the Society to elect its Presidents from staff members of the Department of Theology, rather than automatically appointing the head of the department to the office, and this procedure was adopted in the revised Constitution. The final choice of wording was, 'The President shall be an academic member of staff of the Department of Theology in the University of Hull.'

The committee was reduced from six to four, with power to co-opt not more than three further members, and the quorum was set at four. It was also recognised that the domination of the committee by Anglican clergy had not been a problem for some time, so the sentence in Rule 6, 'It is desirable that not all members be ministers of religion and that the committee should include at least one Roman Catholic, one Jew, and two members of different Protestant bodies', was deleted.

The date of the AGM was to be in 'May or June', and ordinary meetings were in future to follow the academic, not the calendar, year, and would not normally be held during university vacations.

The remaining amendments were small, cosmetic adjustments, giving the committee a little more flexibility in determining the times and places of meetings, and bringing the financial arrangements into line with modern practice.

PROGRAMME 1998-1999
ALTERNATIVE APPROACHES TO THEOLOGY

Wednesday, 21 October, 1998
    The Revd. Jim Jones, Director of the Institute for Community Theology and Religious Heritage, York, *Community Theology.*

Wednesday, 2 December
    Extraordinary General Meeting, followed by Dr Adrian Worsfold, Research Student in the Department of Theology, Hull University, *The Hull Unitarian Church; historical and sociological perspectives.*

Tuesday, 2 February, 1999
    The Rt. Revd. Dr David Tustin, Bishop of Grimsby, *The Devlopment of Anglican-Lutheran relations in the twentieth century.*

Wednesday, 17 March
    The Revd. Dr Michael Wilson, Methodist Minister at Hessle, *Philosophical Theology.*

Saturday, 1 May
    Dr June Boyce-Tillman, King Alfred's College, Winchester, *Hildegard of Bingen: theology and mysticism,* followed by the AGM.

Reaching for the Sky

The first programme of the resurrected Society was issued on a typewritten sheet, but 1999-2000 saw a return to a printed card, this time in an optimistic sky-blue.

    The season was launched on 10 November 1999 with a reception in the Common Room of the Graduate Research Institute, followed by a lecture given by the Revd. Dr Judith Maltby, Fellow, Tutor in History, and Chaplain of Corpus Christi College, Oxford, and a distinguished author. Her subject concerned the implications for modern ecumenical relations of recent scholarship on the English Reformation.

    On 25 November, the Revd. Anthony Bash, Vicar of All Saints Church, North Ferriby, and Honorary Lecturer in New Testament at Hull University, presented a paper entitled *A psychodynamic approach to the interpretation of II Corinthians 10-13* – a scientific reading of Paul's attempt to explain why he appeared to be violent on paper but friendly in personal contact! The talk, which had had to be postponed from the previous session, produced a lively debate.

    Though aware of controversy over the true date of the Millennium, the Society decided to celebrate it on 15 December 1999: 'We believe that any excuse for a party is justified, and so members of the committee have kindly undertaken to provide mincepies and wine for the occasion,' commented the President in a letter to the membership.

The meeting took place in a large lecture theatre in the Ferens Building, adding to the sense of occasion, and Dr David Hughes, Reader in Astronomy at Sheffield University, fought his way through a West Yorkshire blizzard to deliver his illustrated lecture: *The Star of Bethlehem: an astronomer's thoughts.*

* * * *

In January 2000, bad luck hit the Society: Dr Philip Lewis, of Leeds, was obliged to postpone his lecture on Christian-Muslim relationships, and the President, Dr David Bagchi, who was due to step into the breach with a talk on *The Concept of Heresy,* slipped on an icy road and broke a leg, so the meeting scheduled for 19 January had to be cancelled.

Though recovery was slow and painful, that did not deter the President from continuing to work for the Society, and he was present on 16 February, when the long-standing tradition of holding a Students' Evening was revived. The Revd. Ralph Werrell, of Kenilworth, spoke about the thesis he was writing on William Tyndale, and Society Secretary Barbara Robinson told the story of the Hull German Lutheran Church, the subject of her MA dissertation.

President David also overcame his temporary disability to launch a biannual newsletter – THEOLOGIA – a completely new venture for the Society, providing a window on the whole theological scene in the area. It not only gave reviews of past Society events and advance notice of those to come, but also advertised the Annual Chaplaincy Lecture organised by the University of Lincolnshire and Humberside – then Hull University's next-door neighbour – gave details of the newly set-up Kierkegaard Reading Group and publicised the Theology Department's part-time study course.

Continuing the lecture-series, on 1 March the Revd. Canon Dr Martyn Percy, of Sheffield University, presented his lecture, *'Reading the Times', religion and spirituality in a secular age.*

And 6 May 2000 was the date of the Theology Day School, held this year in the Basil Reckitt Theatre of the Ferens Building, when the theme was *Issues in Contemporary Christian Ethics,* and the speakers Dr Bernard Hoose, of Heythrop College, London, and Paul Dearey, Hull University's Lecturer in Social Ethics.

Annual General Meetings were now being held at the close of the Saturday Day Schools, and on 6 May 2000 the President paid tribute to the late Bishop Bill Westwood, who had been a stalwart member of the Society.

It was announced that the Society would shortly have an Internet website, and that the first two Hull Theological Papers had now been published – the Bishop of Grimsby's lecture on Anglican-Lutheran relations and Dr Adrian Worsfold's lecture on the history of the Hull Unitarian Church.

A number of meetings had been arranged for the 2000-2001 season, and it was agreed that Rodney Ward's suggestion of an 'Any Questions?' panel should be pursued. The President also suggested an outing, possibly a tour of local monasteries.

Treasurer Linda Richards said that the Society had begun, and ended, the year with nearly £200. The seven speakers had contributed generously, only one asking for a small fee, the others being satisfied with 'petrol expenses'. The number of paid-up members was 10 more than last year. She suggested that, as a security measure, those attending meetings should be asked to sign in, and it was agreed that a book should be provided for this purpose.

An offer by Paul Dearey to serve as Auditor was gratefully accepted; and Rosa Brown was elected to the committee, bringing it up to strength for the first time since the Society's re-launch.

PROGRAMME 1999-2000

Wednesday, 10 November, 1999
  Reception followed by The Revd. Dr Judith Maltby, Fellow and Chaplain, Corpus Christi College, Oxford, *Recent Scholarship on the English Reformation and its ecumenical implications.*

Thursday, 25 November
  The Revd. Dr Anthony Bash, Vicar of All Saints Church, North Ferriby, Hon. Lecturer in New Testament, Hull University, *A psychodynamic approach to the interpretation of II Corinthians 10-13.*

Wednesday, 15 December
  MILLENNIUM LECTURE. Dr David Hughes, Reader in Astronomy, Sheffield University, *The Star of Bethlehem: an astronomer's thoughts.*

Wednesday, 19 January, 2000
  Meeting cancelled.

Wednesday, 16 February
  Brief presentations on their current research by graduate students of the Theology Department, the Revd. Ralph Werrell and Barbara Robinson.

Wednesday, 1 March
  The Revd. Canon Dr Martyn Percy, Director, Lincoln Theological Institute for Religion and Society, Sheffield University, *'Reading the Times': religion and spirituality in a secular age.*

Saturday, 6 May
  Theology Day School and AGM of the Society. *Issues in Contemporary Christian Ethics:* Dr Bernard Hoose, Lecturer in Pastoral Studies and Head of Development, Heythrop College, London, and Paul Dearey, Lecturer in Social Ethics and Director of the MA in the Theological Understanding of Contemporary Society, Hull University.

Under threat

When the committee met at the University on 2 June 2000, the most serious item on the agenda was the threat of closure confronting the Department of Theology. The University Council had met the previous day and approved plans by the 'Way Forward Group' which envisaged the discontinuation of the Theology programme. Details were given of the proposals affecting the Department, and correspondence was seen, indicating that some negotiation was possible. The matter was fully discussed, and the committee expressed unanimous disapproval of the proposal to close the Department. A letter to the Vice-Chancellor, putting the Society's views forward, was drawn up by the committee and signed by the Secretary.

Meanwhile, it was agreed to proceed with the programme as arranged, and to invite Doctors Lionel and Wendy North to be the speakers at the Saturday Day School.

Linda Richards resigned from the Treasurership, but Fiona Bagchi volunteered to take over the office and her offer was gladly accepted.

Attendances over the past year had been quite good, and it was decided to continue to try to reach interested parties by extending the mailing list.

* * * *

The vexatious situation concerning the future of Theology at Hull University was clearly set out in the December 2000 issue of THEOLOGIA:

'The future of the BA (Hons) degree programme in Theology at Hull University is currently being considered by the University's Academic Portfolio team. This follows the report of the 'Way Forward Group' which advises that the programme should be discontinued.

'Since the chief aim of the Society is to promote the study of Theology at the University, the committee wrote to the Vice-Chancellor, and to the Chair of Council, expressing its concern on behalf of the Society. The Vice-Chancellor replied that no decision to discontinue Theology had yet been taken. It was, however, reported to us by our Patron, the Archbishop of York, that the VC had already apprised him of his belief that the programme was no longer viable.

'At the time of going to press, no decision had been taken. It seems certain, however, that the University's part-time undergraduate programmes [Cert.Theol., Dip.Theol., and B.Th.(Hons)] will continue, as will its post-graduate degrees. Indeed a new part-time postgraduate diploma in Continuing Ministerial and Lay Education will begin this year.'

* * * *

THEOLOGIA also contained news that the first two Hull Theological Papers were now available, containing the text of papers read to the Society or to the Theological Department which had not been published elsewhere: they were:

The development of Anglican-Lutheran ecumenical relations in the 20th century, by the Rt. Revd. Dr David Tustin, Bishop of Grimsby; and *The Hull Unitarian Church: historical and sociological perspectives*, by Dr Adrian Worsfold.

* * * *

The Society now had its own website, on *www.hull.ac.uk/theol/hdts* thanks to the generosity of the Department's webmaster, Ann Broadbent. The pages gave an account of the Society, and a brief history, and the website also carried news of last-minute changes to the annual programme – something extremely valuable, as has been seen, in view of the problems arising from the fact that speakers had to be booked far in advance – and an electronic version of the newsletter.

* * * *

Donations of books by Dr Wendy Sproston North, Mr Jonathan Parker and Dr Daniel and Mrs Vivienne Mariau had enabled the Theology Department to set up a small lending library, primarily for the benefit of Theology undergraduates and THEOLOGIA appealed for further gifts. The collection had been named The North Library in recognition of Wendy's generosity and as a fitting tribute to both Doctors North.

'The North Library offers a valuable service to our undergraduates, particularly by providing duplicate copies of set texts and other frequently consulted titles.'

Pressure works!

There was 'relatively good news' when the committee met on 26 January 2001. The President reported that the University Council had met in December and had approved a plan which did not specify the discontinuation of the Theology degree.

'This indicated that the University clearly responded to external pressure. The axe had fallen elsewhere – on languages, engineering and Asian studies, where staff losses of 50% were expected in the next three years. But even here, external pressure had saved some languages from extinction: action such as students making a noise outside while the Council meeting was taking place.' Staff had put up posters, and the Dutch Ambassador happened to visit Hull to make an award to the Dutch Department! 'All this showed the effectiveness of outside representations.'

Membership of the Society was now 25, compared with the previous year's figure of 29, the highest since 1990-1991, when it was 32, but there was still a long way to go to get back to the situation of the mid-1980s – 43.

Although numbers attending meetings had fallen slightly, the atmosphere was a lot better, largely due to the provision of refreshments, and speakers had commented on this.

Ideas for further publicity were discussed. Notices of meetings were being placed in the *Hull Daily Mail* which provided a free service, and Rodney Ward offered to supply additional names and addresses from the Annual Chaplaincy Lecture mailing list. The proposed programme for 2001-2002 was approved, and Rodney Ward suggested adding a talk on Feminist Theology. The committee also agreed to a joint meeting with Hull Branch of the Classical Association to hear a lecture by Dr Keith Elliott, of Leeds, on the Papyri of the New Testament.

To avoid bank charges, it was agreed to transfer the Society's account to an in-credit free banking society account provided by Lloyds TSB, and to ask for reimbursement of fees already paid.

It was reported that Hull City Vision was approaching various bodies concerned with education, to seek their co-operation in combating the lack of interest in learning shown by many young people in Hull. It was felt that the Society might help in the promotion of religious education, perhaps by running Saturday Day Schools on a more regular basis. It was agreed in principle that the Society should look into the possibility of providing a forum for local teachers of Religious Studies, and that the President should pursue the matter further.

'Excellent!'

A THEOLOGIA EXTRA issued in April 2001 proclaimed 'Theology at Hull University has had the quality of its teaching declared "excellent" by the national review body for higher education.' After a four-day visit by a Quality Assurance Agency review team, the Theology Department was given a score of 23 out of 24. A score of 22 is generally considered to equate to excellence. 'Picked out for special praise by the QAA assessors was the high quality, research-led teaching, the cordial relations between staff and students, and the extent to which students' views informed the teaching provision.

Dr David Bagchi, Director of Theology and President of the Society, said, 'It is good to be told what we always knew. In Theology at Hull and in Religious Studies at Scarborough we have excellent students and excellent staff. In research Theology was awarded a 4 rating in the last Research Assessment Exercise – and now, in teaching, we have demonstrated that we punch far above our weight in enhancing the University's reputation. That's value for money!'

Did this mean that the Department of Theology and its daughter Society were well and truly off the hook? Time would tell!

Progress

At the AGM on 19 May 2001, the President reported that the Society's progress had been satisfactory in every respect. The programme had been completed with no omissions or problems and was very enjoyable. There had been an average of 25 attenders at every meeting, with 22 student attenders over the year. Active membership, excluding students, was 30, comparing well with the previous year.

'All papers had been given by acknowledged experts in their fields – but they had been very interesting and exciting as well,' said Dr Bagchi. 'It was no easy task to combine scholarship with accessibility, but all speakers have done that. They were appreciative of the audience participation, and went away with new ideas to add to their studies.'

The atmosphere of the meetings was very much better, thanks to the provision of refreshments. The President thanked the Secretary, and also paid tribute to the former Treasurer, Linda Richards, saying that through her energy and persistence she had helped to maintain the Society's finances, generating a surplus which allowed it to range far afield for speakers and to defray their travelling costs.

The acting-Hon.Treasurer, Fiona Bagchi, reported that income had been up on the previous year (£405.61 against £377), but speakers' expenses were higher (£360 against £271) leaving a surplus of £45.61. The General Fund stood at £246.87. Thanks were expressed to Fiona for her services and she was formally elected Hon.Treasurer. Prof. L. L. Grabbe proposed a vote of thanks to the President and Mrs Bagchi, saying that they had worked very hard to keep the Society going.

PROGRAMME 2000-2001

Wednesday, 18 October, 2000
   In the Leslie Downs Theatre, Ferens Building
   Gaye Ortiz, University College of Ripon and York St. John, *Jesus, Mary and Joseph, (Holy) family values in film* (with film clips).

Wednesday, 15 November
   In the Leslie Downs Theatre, Ferens Building
   Dr Philip Lewis, Leeds University, *From diatribe to dialogue: the depiction of Christianity by Muslim institutions in Britain.*

Wednesday, 6 December
   Anne Overell, The Open University, Yorkshire Region, *The English Reformation and the Italian Connection.*

Wednesday, 17 January, 2001
   Dr Linda Woodhead, Senior Lecturer in the Department of Religious Studies, Lancaster University, *Soft Religion: the spiritual revolution of our times.*

Wednesday, 21 February
   Dr James Ginther, Department of Theology and Religious Studies, Leeds University, *The concept of 'sola scriptura' in medieval theology.*

Wednesday, 21 March
   Prof. Alan Ford, Nottingham Univeristy, *The Pope as Antichrist: reading the Book of Revelation in Ireland.*

Saturday, 19 May
> Joint HDTS/Theology Department Day School and Society AGM: Dr Lionel North and Dr Wendy Sproston North, Durham, *'Who is this man, that even the wind and the sea obey him?'* Is Jesus God?

Great Dane?

The Society's 44th season was launched with a talk on 23 October 2001 by Dr Steven Shakespeare, who completed his doctorate on Kierkegaard at Cambridge, and who undertook to tackle the question of the pessimistic 19th-century Danish writer's continuing relevance for present-day Christian faith.

Writing in the October 2001 issue of THEOLOGIA, President David Bagchi could not resist the piquant headline, 'Shakespeare's anguished Dane'!

'Søeren Kierkegaard is not easy to pigeon-hole into any particular tradition,' he wrote. 'He was especially critical of the Danish Lutheranism in which he was brought up – but for that reason his thinking has survived the last 150 years better than most.'

The first committee meeting of the session was held over lunch at the Garden Palace Chinese Restaurant on 24 October. The reason for this congenial venue was that it made a pleasant setting for a farewell to Rodney and Judith Ward, who were to leave shortly for Berwick-on-Tweed. Thanks were expressed to them for their support of the Society, and gifts were presented. It was hoped that they might eventually return to Hull and rejoin the Society. Plans were also completed for the forthcoming visit of the Society's Patron, the Archbishop of York.

Another highlight of 2000-2001 was *The Christmas story in stained glass,* told by Peter Gibson, OBE, maker and restorer of stained glass, most notably at York Minster, where he was responsible for making good the extensive damage following the fire in 1984.

And in February 2002, the Society's first *'Any Theological Questions?'* took place, with Pat Doyle, former Leader of Hull City Council, and a prominent member of Hull's Roman Catholic community, the Bishop of Hull, the Rt. Revd. Richard Frith, Dr Hugh Pyper, Head of Theology and Religious Studies at Leeds University (and a Quaker), and Ann Eccleston, a graduate of Hull University and long-serving member of the Society, who stepped in at the last minute in place of Heather Clark, of Hull Council for Voluntary Service, who was unable to be present.

The panel was recruited by the Secretary and by the Revd. Rodney Ward, who was unable to chair the meeting as planned, because he had already left the city to take up his new appointment, so the President stepped into the breach. Despite these setbacks, the experiment was voted 'an enterprising departure from the usual meetings'. And there were calls for it to be repeated.

* * * *

The Seminar Room in the University's Graduate Research Institute may not have been able to compete with the Garden Palace Restaurant for elegance, but it was proving a most suitable place for the Society's meetings. Large enough to accommodate a fair-sized audience – extra chairs had to be brought in for the Archbishop's visit – it was small enough to be friendly and intimate, and did not 'swallow up' a modest gathering, as seemed to happen when a large lecture theatre was booked.

The only snag was the security-door, which had to be manned in order to let the audience in before the start of the meeting, but this was a small price to pay for the free use of such a pleasant and otherwise-accessible home-base. The large halls in the nearby Ferens Building were used for the more ambitious presentations, when slides or films were involved, but these had to be paid for, and, as mentioned, were too big for the average Society audience.

At a meeting of the committee on 19 March 2002, it was agreed that there had been some splendid meetings, including the visit of the Archbishop, whose lecture was to be included in the series of published papers. Attendances at the earlier events had been sparse, but numbers had picked up again after Peter Gibson's talk on stained glass, though they had fallen after that. However, similar organisations such as the Classical Association were experiencing the same problems. The President said that he was 'warning speakers what to expect, and some responded well'. Publicity was again discussed, and Linda Richards suggested making a special effort in Cottingham, as it was near the University. Treasurer Fiona Bagchi submitted an account showing a sum of £547.88 in the bank.

Land of Conflict

The theme of the Theology Day School, run jointly this year by the Society and the Theology Department, was *The Bible, Archaeology and History,* and was held in the Wilberforce Building on 25 May 2002.

The preamble to the programme is still sadly topical: 'As the Palestinian *intifada* and the Israeli "war against terror" rage on, we are reminded that both the land over which they fight and the Hebrew Scriptures/Old Testament are revered, in different ways, by the three religions involved.'

Questions dealt with included, 'Can the Bible be relied on to give us a true record of the extent of ancient Israel's power and territory?' 'Does archaeology confirm or confute the historical accuracy of the Bible, and should archaeologists be motivated by such questions?' and 'Have Israelis, Jordanians and others promoted archaeology merely as a continuation of war by other means?'

These subjects, and more, were considered by Prof. P. R. Davies, of the Department of Biblical Studies, Sheffield University, and Prof. L. L. Grabbe, Director of Hull's Graduate Research Institute and author of many books and articles.

* * * *

At the AGM, the President announced the untimely death of Dr Obi Igwara, to whom he paid tribute. The departure of Rodney and Judith Ward had also been a loss to the Society, but was a gain to their new church in Berwick-on-Tweed.

Once again the Society had enjoyed a series of varied and interesting meetings. The Red Letter Day was the Patronal visit of the Archbishop of York, Dr David Hope.

Average attendance at the previous year's meetings was 23, but this was almost entirely due to the Archbishop's visit. Numbers at this year's meetings had been disappointing, averaging 17. Was there any way the speakers and events could be made more interesting? Linda Richards thought that the poor attendance was no reflection on the speakers, but was due to lack of publicity. Was it possible to use the local press more? She also felt that the Society was 'hidden away' at the University. The President replied that the best events took place across 'exam time', and suggested that the dates might be changed to avoid this period. Dr Elfride Bickersteth suggested that the Theology Day School might be held in the winter, to avoid spending the time indoors on a pleasant summer day. Other ideas included arranging joint meetings with other organisations such as the Historical Society, holding more evening meetings in the summer, or timing them to coincide with University events. It was left to the committee to explore these possibilities.

Treasurer Fiona Bagchi presented her report, showing a surplus for the year of £249.71, giving net assets of £496.58. Linda Richards thought the £65 hotel bill for one speaker was too high, and offered to provide overnight accommodation at her own establishment at a concessionary £15 per person – including transport!

The President, Secretary and committee members Canon L. S. Deas, Linda Richards and Mary Rose Kearney had completed their terms of office, but were willing to be nominated for re-election. All were returned to office:

President, Dr. David Bagchi, proposed by Canon Deas, seconded by Prof. Grabbe.

Secretary, Barbara Robinson, proposed by Dr Bickersteth seconded by Canon Deas.

Committee members Canon Deas, Linda Richards and Mary Rose Kearney were proposed *en bloc* by the Revd. David Coote, seconded by Rosa Brown. Linda Richards proposed the election of the Revd. David Coote to replace the Revd. Rodney Ward on the committee. This was seconded by Canon Deas and approved.

PROGRAMME 2001-2002

Tuesday, 23 October, 2001
    The Revd. Dr Steven Shakespeare, Sheffield University, *On not being whole: Kierkegaard's importance for Christian faith.*

Wednesday, 14 November
> Dr Tony Dodd, Course Co-ordinator for Religious Studies at the Scarborough Campus of Hull University, *Academic life towards the end of the thirteenth century.*

Tuesday, 11 December
> Mr Peter Gibson OBE, York, *The Christmas story in stained glass.*

Thursday, 24 January, 2002
> The Most Revd. Dr David Hope, Archbishop of York, *Liturgy and Worship – Fixed or Flexible?*

Tuesday, 19 February
> 'Any Theological Questions?', with Pat Doyle, former Leader of Hull City Council, The Rt. Revd. Richard Frith, Bishop of Hull, Dr Hugh Pyper, Head of the Department of Theology and Religious Studies, Leeds University, and Ann Eccleston, deputising for Heather Clark, Hull Council for Voluntary Service. Chairman, Dr David Bagchi, President of the Society.

Wednesday, 13 March
> The Revd. Melvin Tinker, Hull, *Last Supper/Lord's Supper: more than a parable in action?*

Tuesday, 16 April
> Dr Santha Bhattacharji, Keble College, Oxford, *The Book of Margery Kempe.*

Saturday, 25 May
> Joint Society and Theology Department Day School with Prof. P. R. Davies, Sheffield University, and Prof. L. L. Grabbe, Hull University, *The Bible, Archaeology and History.*

Knox to Tango!

Introducing the 2002-2003 programme, THEOLOGIA opened in reflective mood:

'Forgiveness and reconciliation have been much in the news lately, the most astonishing example being the work of the Truth and Reconciliation Commission in South Africa. The question of reparation, for grievances perhaps centuries old, has also come to the fore: for example, over whether certain African countries should be recompensed for the West's historic involvement in the slave trade. But is a "proxy" forgiveness by the aggrieved party's descendants possible? Forgiveness has become a matter of politics as much as of ethics.'

Helping the Society through this moral maze on 16 October 2002 was Prof. Nigel Biggar, of Leeds, who titled his talk *Who may forgive and when?*

In November, the Society welcomed Dr Ian Hazlett, Reader in Church History at the University of Glasgow, who delivered a lecture on *Mary Stuart and John Knox on religious freedom and toleration.* 'Neither the Queen of Scots nor the Berwick preacher was noted for tolerance so we can expect an eye-opening evening,' predicted THEOLOGIA. And so it proved.

Christmas card imagery is a powerful, if little-regarded, conveyor of folk beliefs and sentiments, as well as of commercial values, and this was the subject of the Christmas lecture given by Dr Gavin White, of St Andrews. Once again, this seasonable event was accompanied by wine and mincepies.

In January 2003, Dr Julian Haseldine, of Hull University's Department of History, challenged current views on the degree to which medieval citizens regarded themselves as individuals and how far Christians were discouraged from regarding themselves as other than members of a larger body.

And in February, Dr Julian Stern, also from the 'home--university', accompanied his lecture, *Community, Schools and Religion* with a multi-page handout in which he had this to say about his adopted city:

'Hull is a city with more sense of self, more of a sense of its own distinctiveness, than any city I have known. Hull combines this sense of self with a kind of friendliness and a tight network of relationships that would in most circumstances be called "social capital".'

But, he added, Hull's very closeness was a worry, because it was all too rarely exploited: 'My own image of Hull is of a city having a huge quantity of social capital that it hides under a mattress,' he wrote. Dr Stern's campaign to find that mattress and invest its contents was explained in a deeply philosophical paper encompassing life, death – and education!

Moving from an entertaining if profound dissertation to one which, on the surface, appeared mainly entertaining, the Society was transported into a cinematic extravaganza in which Dr Lesley Coote explored the hidden moral depths to be found in the classic adventure film, *El Cid,* and even those who had seen it more than once enjoyed re-living the magnificent battle-scenes and moving climax.

There was yet another climax to the year as Prof. Tim Macquiban, of Salisbury, delivered the Wesley Tercentenary Lecture commemorating the 300th anniversary of the birth of the Founder of Methodism.

Religion and the Arts was the theme of the May Theology Day School, led by Dr Daniel Mariau, of Hull University, and the Revd. Paul Burkitt.

'From prehistoric times, humans have tried to make sense of their lives through art and through religion,' the programme recalled. 'Through both they have expressed their conviction of a deeper dimension of reality.'

At times the two had walked hand in hand, but at other times the representation – or mis-representation – of divine things had outraged the iconoclasts, while some of the most devastating attacks on religion had been made by artists.

Paul Burkitt explored the relationship between art and spirituality while Daniel Mariau, after illustrating the complexities and meaning of sacred architecture in the Hindu temple, used film to illustrate how the Latin

Americans had come to regard the Tango as a religious rite.

* * * *

Past and future

In his report to the AGM, the President emphasised the wide variety of subjects which had been covered over the year:

'What other society in Hull could have brought together in one place the Holocaust and Medieval Monasteries, Mary Queen of Scots and John Wesley, John Knox and the Tango?' he asked. Local speakers had played a valuable part, and thanks were due to members who had turned out in all weathers to support the Society. Tributes were paid to two former members who had died, Trevor Silverwood and Josephina Donald.

Next year would see the 50th anniversary of the foundation of the University's Department of Theology, which would be followed by that of the Society itself in 2007. It was proposed to invite past and present staff members of the Department to talk about their work, which would cover a wide range of theology, embracing 50 years of scholarship in various areas, and also take a look into the future.

Geoffrey Sharps had recorded the talks given at the Theology Day School and agreed to supply tapes to the Society. He suggested that lectures should be regularly taped for the record, and that a history of the Society should be compiled.

The Treasurer reported that income was just over £100 down on the previous year, mainly due to a drop in subscriptions. Expenditure was higher because several speakers had come long distances, involving travel and overnight accommodation. However, the balance in the bank at the end of the year was £445.39, little more than £50 down on the previous year. She suggested that efforts should be made to increase the number of subscription-paying members, and that programmes should be sent out earlier.

The President pointed out that students were automatically members of the Society, but many were unable to attend because they had jobs. When a lecture was of direct relevance to a student, he or she might make a special effort to come. Linda Richards agreed to collect payments from non-members attending lectures, and suggested that a flyer should be produced for circulation to churches and displayed in appropriate places to inform the public of the activities of the Society.

Rosa Brown, whose term of office had ended, nominated Ann Eccleston to take her place on the committee. This was seconded by Elfride Bickersteth and agreed.

It was, in short, a year in which theological heights had been scaled, but, as always, the minutiae of organisational efficiency had not been neglected.

PROGRAMME 2002-2003

Wednesday, 16 October, 2002
   Prof. Nigel Biggar, Department of Theology and Religious Studies, Leeds University, *Who may forgive what, and when?*

Wednesday, 13 November
   Dr Ian Hazlett, Department of Church History, Glasgow University, *Mary Stuart and John Knox on Religious Freedom and Toleration.*

Wednesday, 11 December
   Dr Gavin White, St.Andrews (former Reader in Divinity, Glasgow University), *Christmas cards, the images and their development.*

Wednesday, 15 January, 2003
   Dr Julian Haseldine, Department of History, Hull University, *Medieval Monasticism and the Discovery of the Individual.*

Wednesday, 12 February
   Dr Julian Stern, Centre For Educational Studies, Hull University, *Community, Schools and Religion.*

Wednesday, 12 March
   Dr Lesley Coote, Lecturer in English, Hull University, *The representation of the Crusades and the construction of the oriental 'other' in such Hollywood films of the 1960s as 'El Cid'.*

Wednesday, 30 April
   Prof. Tim Macquiban, Principal of Sarum College, Salisbury, former Director of the Centre for Wesley Studies, the Westminster Institute, Oxford Brookes University, *The Wesley Tercentenary Lecture.*

Saturday, 23 May
   The Hull Theology Day School, organised by the Department of Humanities: Theology, and the Hull & District Theological Society, *Religion and the Arts,* with Dr Daniel Mariau, Lecturer in Indic Religions and the Philosophy of Religion, Hull University, and the Revd. Paul Burkitt, Priest-in-Charge, St Mary's, Lowgate, Hull, one of the Archbishop of York's Chaplains in the Arts in the North East.

Year of Jubilee

In 2003-2004, the Society shared fully in the Theology Department's celebrations of half-a-century of teaching and research. The links had never been stronger.

The Society's entire programme was made up of lectures by staff members of the Department, each featuring his own special field of study. The only tragic note was struck by the sudden death of Prof. Anthony Monti, who was to have been the one visiting speaker of the season. There was no time to find a substitute, or even to cancel the meeting, so Secretary Barbara Robinson filled in with a progress report on the compilation of this history of the Society.

THEOLOGIA appeared in October 2003, highlighting the achievements of the Department, summarising the earlier lecture, and giving a foretaste of those to come.

The Theology Day School on the theme of *Jesus and Paul: The End of the Law?* on 23 February 2004 provided further opportunity for co-operation. Led by Prof. Morna Hooker, of Cambridge University, who also gave the Jubilee Lecture, *Paul and the Atonement,* the same day, the programme included contributions by Prof. Lester Grabbe the Revd. Dr. Anthony Bash, Mr Paul Dearey and the Society's President, Dr David Bagchi.

At the Annual General Meeting on 10 May 2004, it was reported that attendances were down, possibly because the speakers were well known to Society members, but the programme planned for the following year would be back to normal, with a varied mixture of local and 'distant' speakers.

Treasurer Fiona Bagchi reported a 'swings-and-roundabouts' situation: the fact that all the lecturers had been from Hull meant that there were no speakers' expenses, and other costs were borne by the Department as part of the 50th Anniversary celebrations so the balance now stood at £684.13. But there was a need to address the continued fall in the subscribing membership, which had halved in two years from more than 30 in 2002 to 16 this year:

'However, the reason for the fall may simply be that this year's speakers, being from Hull and having been heard by members many times before, did not attract audiences, and that income will return to normal next year, when the programme once again includes visiting speakers. We now have a large enough fund to afford the travel expenses of several such speakers and to have a reasonable reserve in case of emergencies.'

* * * *

The AGM was followed by An Evening of Scandinavian Theology, organised by the Department of Humanities: Theology, in association with the Society

The speakers, Prof. Jens Glebe-Møller, formerly of Copenhagen University, Dr Rosemary Køhn, Bishop of Hamar Stift, Norway, and Dr Susanne Sonderbø, also from Hamar, were recruited by the Revd. Hjørdis Kjaergaard, Pastor of the Hull Danish Church, which was also celebrating the Golden Jubilee of its Osborne Street building.

A buffet supper in the Staff House, on the University campus, completed a memorable evening.

PROGRAMME 2003-2004

Wednesday, 15 October 2003
   The Revd. Dr. Anthony Bash (Hon. Director of New Testament Studies, University of Hull), *A psychological approach to the theology of forgiveness.*

Wednesday, 19 November
> Mr Paul Dearey (Lecturer in Christian Doctrine and Ethics, University of Hull), *The contextual and the corporate: recent developments in Christian theology.*

Wednesday, 17 December
> Prof. Lester Grabbe (Professor of Hebrew Bible and Early Judaism, University of Hull), *'The history of Israel': retrospect and prospects.*

Wednesday, 21 January, 2004
> (Advertised speaker, Prof. Anthony Monti, *Anticipating the new creation: the arts as inherently theological.* Owing to the sudden death of Prof. Monti shortly before the meeting, Barbara Robinson gave a résumé of work done on the history of the Society.)

Wednesday, 18 February
> Dr David Bagchi (Lecturer in the History of Christian Thought, University of Hull), *Martin Luther, 1954-2004: the reformer reformed.*

Monday, 23 February
> THE JUBILEE LECTURE: Prof Morna Hooker (Robinson College, Cambridge), *Paul and the Atonement.*

Wednesday, 17 March
> Dr Daniel Mariau (Lecturer in Indian Religions, University of Hull), *DO; the Japanese acculturation of a Buddhist theme.*

Monday, 10 May
> AGM followed by An Evening of Scandinavian Theology, with Professor Jens Glebe-Møller, of the University of Copenhagen, Dr Rosemary Køhn, Bishop of Hamar Stift, and Dr Susanne Sonderbø, also of Hamar.-

THEOLOGY DAY SCHOOL 2004
Monday, 23 February, 10.30 am – 4.00 pm
Jesus and Paul: the End of the Law?

Working together

The 2004-2005 season was remarkably successful, despite the fact that President David Bagchi, on whom so much of the responsibility for providing quality speakers depended, was taking a sabbatical which required him to spend a considerable amount of time in Oxford. The committee pulled together, however, and, although they met only once, on 26 July 2004, the plans made at that meeting carried the programme through, the difficulties being surmounted as they arose.

The committee met in the beautiful garden of Mary Rose Kearney's home in Park Avenue, Hull, and one of the topics which came up was the question of why the lectures did not appeal more strongly to local clergy. Should not a serious theological debate prove stimulating to a trained mind all too often confined to coping with the day-to-day emotional and religious needs of ordinary parishioners? After all, the founders had been afraid that the Society might become 'an exclusive club for Anglican clergy'!

The discussion, however, revealed the changing pattern of clerical life since the Society was founded: despite falling church attendances, ministers were now extremely pressured, especially with hospital chaplaincy work, which often involved going deeply into theological issues, and most felt the need for a complete break in their limited leisure time.

Publicity was to be stepped up, and it was hoped that this, in conjunction with an ambitious programme – made possible by the financial savings of the previous year – would attract higher attendances

Time-tables

Speakers proved ready and willing to come to Hull, but several had to delay giving a firm date until they had received their time-tables for the year. This seemed to be a nation-wide phenomenon affecting all the universities, and it was the sole reason why it had been impossible to produce a printed programme until the series had got under way – a considerable inconvenience, since most supporters needed to get dates into their diaries in good time.

Nevertheless, there were creditable numbers present at the early meetings. The first took place just three days before Hallowe'en, and, as the theme of the lecture was *The problem of* the *ghost in the Middle Ages,* members were hardly surprised to be greeted by a pumpkin lantern, a flying bat and a collection of ghoulish-looking but tasty nibbles.

The Revd. Professor David Crouch said that, although St Augustine had ruled that Christians were not supposed to believe that departed spirits might haunt the earth, ghost stories abounded in the Middle Ages, and he gave a number of examples. Happily, the Society's Honorary Members, Doctors Lionel and Wendy North, who now lived in Darlington, were present in body as well as spirit to help launch the new season.

Wine and mincepies graced the table at the December meeting, and the lecture once more had a seasonable theme: *Apparitions of the Blessed Virgin Mary.* Dr Chris Maunder reminded members that Mary had been the subject of renewed scholarly interest in recent years, not least through the activities of the Centre for Marian Studies of which he was a leading member. This, in fact, was only one of the topics in which the Society's programme anticipated newscasts which were to feature in the general media later in the year.

* * * *

The theme explored at the Theology Day School in February was *Early Christianity and Judaism: the parting of the ways.* The event took place in the Staff House on the Hull campus, and was led by Professor Lester Grabbe, of the home university, and John Barclay, the newly-appointed Lightfoot Professor of New Testament at the University of Durham. The process of separation and self-definition for both religions was shown to be no simple matter. The two faiths criss-crossed many times in many ways before a definite dichotomy could be discerned.

In the news

The issue of blasphemy had been much in the news in the spring of 2005, following the BBC's decision to screen *Jerry Springer: The Opera,* and the ensuing protests of a vociferous Christian pressure group. The Government was also attempting to enact legislation outlawing incitement to religious hatred.

At the Society's February meeting, Dr Bagchi showed how the charge of 'blasphemy' was adopted by English Protestants as a more ecumenical concept than the old charge of heresy, and how some current issues had their echoes in the past. The fact that the President's sabbatical research included the preparation of a monograph on the concept of heresy in early-modern England and Germany lent further topicality to the lecture.

There was a surprise for the audience at the March meeting, when Dr Richard Andrew was the speaker. Owing to a misunderstanding, he had been expected to talk about the work of the York Institute for Community Theology, of which he was the Director, but instead he delivered a thought-provoking paper on *Karl Barth and the Theology of Mission,* which, though distinctly different, was equally enjoyed and appreciated.

In April, the theme returned to the early development of Protestantism, when Dr Amanda Capern, Lecturer in Women's History at the University of Hull, spoke on *Providence and religious authority in early-modern England,* showing how the people of the time felt the power of divine influence in shaping their lives, and how women had played an important role, especially as letter-writers and diary-keepers.

Owing to a clash of room-bookings, the March and April meetings had to be re-located from the Graduate School to a lecture-room in the Wilberforce Building, but members and guests found their way there through rain, darkness and building-works, and attendance was not affected.

The President produced an excellent spring-time edition of THEOLOGIA, keeping members up-to-date with news of both the Department and the Society.

Shaken – and stirred!

The Revd. Canon Andrew Shanks was described as 'one of the most important and exciting British theologians of our time', and his presence at the Annual General Meeting on 11 May 2005 made a fitting climax to the season.

His chief concern was Christianity's engagement with contemporary society – a complex theme indeed – and it was not until he rose to speak that his final choice of title was revealed: *An Honest Church?* The search for honesty shakes the seeker's ideas: 'The solidarity of Christians, as Christians, is therefore valid precisely to the extent that it's transparent to the solidarity of the shaken. Otherwise it isn't faith, but church ideology.'

The rise of public conscience movements from the 1960s – peace, civil liberties, anti-racist, feminist, green, gay liberation and trade justice – was the nearest thing to a direct organisational expression of the solidarity of the shaken, he declared. His proposed new church calendar would include a Christian Day of Atonement and commemorations of the Holocaust, slavery and the problems of Ireland. Question-time proved how challenging the audience found his views.

The future

As these records indicate, the Society's custom was to hold the business part of the AGM at the beginning of the meeting, with the lecture and discussion as the 'reward' for those who conscientiously stayed the course. On this occasion, however, the speaker was obliged to leave in time to catch the train back to Manchester, so the procedure was reversed.

However, the agenda proved no anticlimax, as it predicted a cautiously optimistic future for the Society. Treasurer Fiona Bagchi reported a 'healthy' bank-balance of £876.63, mainly due to the fact that, once again, a number of the speakers had been local, so that expenses amounted to only £145.90. It was anticipated that the figure would be higher for the coming year. Membership had dropped to 16 the previous year, but had since risen to 24, and it was hoped that it would increase still further.

The retiring officers and committee were all willing to stand again, and were re-elected *en bloc* on a proposition by Dr Elfride Bickersteth, seconded by Professor Lester Grabbe: President, Dr David Bagchi, Secretary, Barbara Robinson, Treasurer, Fiona Bagchi; committee, Canon Stephen Deas, the Revd. David Coote, Mary Rose Kearney, Linda Richards and Ann Eccleston.

Finally, the President presented a list of speakers for the year 2005-2006, showing that all but one of the dates had been filled.

PROGRAMME 2004-2005

Thursday, 28 October, 2004
 The Revd Professor David Crouch (Professor of Medieval History, University of Hull), *The problem of the ghost in the Middle Ages.*
Wednesday, 15 December
 Dr Chris Maunder (Dept. of Theology, College of York St John), *Apparitions of the Blessed Virgin Mary.*
THEOLOGY DAY SCHOOL
Tuesday, 1 February, 2005
 10.00 am – 4.00 pm

Professor John Barclay (Lightfoot Professor of New Testament, University of Durham); Professor Lester Grabbe (Professor of Hebrew Bible and Early Judaism, University of Hull), *Early Christianity and Judaism: separation and reconfiguration.*

Wednesday, 16 February
Dr David Bagchi (Director of Theology, University of Hull), *From heresy to blasphemy: the evolution of an idea in early-modern England and Germany.*

Thursday, 10 March
The Revd. Richard Andrew (Director, York Institute for Community Theology), *Karl Barth and the Theology of Mission.*

Wednesday, 13 April
Dr Amanda Capern, (Lecturer in Women's History, University of Hull), *Providence and religious authority in early-modern England.*

Wednesday, 11 May
ANNUAL GENERAL MEETING.
The Revd. Canon Dr Andrew Shanks (Canon Theologian of Manchester Cathedral), *An Honest Church?*

Moving on

The 2005-2006 season might be described as being 'reflectively satisfying'. Meetings were pleasant and sociable, offering not only mental stimulus but companionable exchange, with a glass of wine to enhance a special occasion.

Attendance was moving upward – an average of 20 per meeting, against 18 the previous year and 16 the year before – modest increases, no doubt, but the Seminar Room in the University's Graduate School always seemed reasonably well occupied, and members were in no hurry to leave at the end of the lecture, often lingering to discuss with the speaker some question they had not been able to put from the 'floor'.

Indeed, the enthusiasm of members for the monthly meetings remained high. At the AGM the President aired the possibility of holding meetings less frequently, perhaps every two months. This would have echoed the practice of the recently re-formed Hull and East Riding Interfaith Group which at its meetings in the Guildhall was at this time attracting larger audiences than the Theological Society. However, the suggestion was met with strong opposition from the floor, and was evidently not put to the vote.

Although he had once again been obliged to spend a great deal of time on research leave, Dr Bagchi had managed to persuade six distinguished scholars to pledge their time and erudition to address the Society, while the custom of holding a 'Students' Evening' had been revived to provide a seventh event.

The only regular feature missing from the programme was the annual

Day School, but at the Annual Meeting the President promised to try to arrange one for the coming year, 'subject to the availability of a speaker'. Opinions were divided as to whether this should be in the summer or the winter.

Patronage

Dr John Sentamu, who had recently succeeded Dr Hope as Archbishop of York, agreed to continue the tradition of becoming the Society's Patron, and it was hoped that in the fullness of time he would be able to make a patronal visit to Hull to address the members.

The return to the practice of engaging lecturers from different parts of the country inevitably made a slight dent in the bank account, but the reserve built up during the previous concentration on local speakers ensured that the Treasurer's report still reflected a comfortable financial situation. Speakers' expenses for the year amounted to £310.09, and door fees were down by £80, creating a deficit of £51.51, with a further £50 cheque still to be cleared, but, with £821.12 in the account, there was no cause for concern.

Topical start

In the spring of 2006, much interest and comment was being engendered by the release of the film of *The Da Vinci Code*. American novelist Dan Brown's fast-moving thriller blended fact, legend and pure invention in an intriguing modern version of the age-old quest for the Holy Grail, implying that the Church might have been responsible for the biggest cover-up in history. Some Christian leaders were concerned that readers or viewers might get perilously lost in this labyrinth of theological theories.

So it was appropriate that the Society's programme should open with a talk by Prof. Loveday Alexander on *Raiders of a Lost Ark? The Bible, the critics and the Da Vinci Code*. It was, she said, fashionable to criticise the book and those who took it too seriously, but at least, by its use of the Gnostic gospels, it brought to public view the process by which the canon of the New Testament was formed, and raised wider questions about how we relate faith and history.

* * * *

At the November meeting, the Revd. Rachel Ganney, a PhD student, asked the question, 'Where was the Holy Spirit during the crucifixion?' An influential answer, she thought, was given by the German theologian Jürgen Moltmann: Although the Son was apparently abandoned by the Father from Good Friday to Easter morning, they were still united by the bond of the Spirit. She wondered if this understanding of the Spirit as instrument did justice to its Personhood.

The second paper came from another PhD student, the Revd. Michael

Willson, who argued that the standard theories of the Atonement ignored the importance of Christ's obedience in Gethsemane and on the cross. This obedience, a model for all Christians, was an important aspect of Paul's thinking that had been submerged by the Catholic emphasis on love and the Protestant emphasis on faith.

The papers were warmly received by the audience, and sparked lively discussions.

* * * *

In December, when the Revd. Jeremy Clines described the situation of the Palestinian Christian community in the West Bank, he found sympathisers who had long been wrestling with the seemingly intractable problems of the Middle East through membership of Hull Council of Christians and Jews, and information flowed between speaker and listener. Clearly moved by his experiences when visiting the area, Mr Clines said that many Palestinian Christians had emigrated, and there were now more of them in the United States than in the disputed territory. The result, however, was that those who remained were even more embattled.

Rise and Fall
When a seemingly good idea ends in failure, it is always puzzling as well as sad, and such a case was the subject of the January meeting. Prof. V. Alan McClelland, a former Professor of Educational Studies at Hull University, told of *The Rise and Fall of Corpus Christi College, London*, a seat of learning set up as a national centre for the training of Catholic teachers in 1966, in the wake of Vatican II. Although it was based on a successful Belgian model, difficulties arose almost immediately.

Shortage of money was an on-going problem, and dioceses were reluctant to send students to London. There were staff problems, too, and, when complaints about the orthodoxy of lectures were made by some extra-mural students, the closure of the college was in sight. It was, however, Prof. McClelland argued, managerial inadequacy rather than theological radicalism that led to the college's demise.

* * * *

The meeting on 1 March was moved to a large lecture hall in the Ferens building, to facilitate the screening by Prof. John Wolffe of detailed tables from *The Religious Census of 1851 in Yorkshire*.

Part of the first national census of modern times, the returns provided uniquely detailed information on patterns of church-going in Victorian Britain. In particular, they showed the effects of the Evangelical Revival and of Catholic Emancipation in eroding the position of the Established

Church. By the mid-19th century, attendances at Methodist and Roman Catholic churches almost equalled Anglican attendances.

This produced problems for the compilers, however: an eager Christian might attend a Methodist class in the early morning preparatory to communion in the parish church, and so be counted twice.

* * * *

Sudden illness brought disappointment on 22 March, not only for the audience, who had been looking forward to a talk by the Revd. Dr Teresa Morgan, Fellow and Tutor in Ancient History at Oriel College, Oxford, on *Bridget Jones's Theology*, but also to the President, who had once been her Sunday School teacher. However, it was hoped that the lecture – and the reunion – would be but briefly deferred, and that members and their friends would soon be listening to Dr Morgan's *Reflections on Involuntary Singleness*.

Stepping into the breach once more, the President gave an enlightening paper on *Catholic Anti-Judaism in Reformation Germany*. This was based on Luther's opponent, Johann Eck, who, in 1541, wrote a defence of the infamous 'blood libel', which had accused the Jews of ritually murdering Christian children. Dr Bagchi argued that Eck, writing at a time when Luther was regarded as Pro-Jewish, saw both Jews and Lutherans as enemies of the church who were wrongly tolerated in the Empire.

Newsletter

Also in March, an issue of the newsletter, THEOLOGIA, was circulated, giving summaries of the lectures already delivered, notice of those to come and information about the Society.

And finally...

At the Annual General Meeting on 10 May, farewells were said to Mary Rose Kearney, who was leaving Hull after many years of service to the Society.

The Revd. Robin McDowall was elected to the committee in her place and Ann Eccleston was elected for a further term. President David Bagchi, Secretary Barbara Robinson and Treasurer Fiona Bagchi remained in office and the committee now consisted of Robin McDowall, Ann Eccleston, David Coote, Stephen Deas and Linda Richards.

The final lecture of the year was *Theology Through Hymns,* in which Dr Ian Bradley illustrated his choice of examples in a rich baritone voice. Most people, he said, learned their theology through hymns: 'They are what stick in people's minds after the service.' Singing hymns to different tunes could alter their theology altogether. Creation and the majesty of God were themes for some of the best-known hymns, but social gospel hymns and even popular musical shows could provide inspiration. 'Hymns should speak to the intellect as well as to the emotions'.

PROGRAMME 2005-2006

Wednesday, 5 October, 2005
> Professor Loveday Alexander (Department of Biblical Studies, University of Sheffield), *Raiders of a Lost Ark? The Bible, the Critics and the Da Vinci Code.*

Wednesday, 9 November
> Students' Evening. The Revd. Rachel Ganney, *The Holy Spirit and the Cross in the works of Moltmann: 'The Crucified God'*. The Revd. Michael Willson, *Loving Obedience and a New Theory of the Atonement.*

Thursday, 8 December
> The Revd Jeremy Clines (Chaplain, College of York St John, York), *'Caught in the Between': the Struggle for Palestinian Christian Identity and Survival in the Occupied Territories.*

Wednesday, 25 January, 2006
> Professor V. A. McClelland (Professor Emeritus of Education, University of Hull), *The Second Vatican Council and the Rise and Fall of Corpus Christi College, London.*

Wednesday, 1 March
> Professor John Wolffe (Professor of Religious History, The Open University), *The Religious Census of 1851 in Yorkshire.*

Wednesday, 22 March
> Dr David Bagchi (Lecturer in the History of Christian Thought, University of Hull), *Catholic Anti-Semitism in Reformation Germany: The Case of Johann Eck.*

Wednesday, 10 May
> ANNUAL GENERAL MEETING
> The Revd. Dr Ian Bradley (Reader in Practical Theology, University of St Andrews), *Theology through Hymns.*

Faith and Freedom

It was a happy coincidence that the Society's 50th anniversary coincided with the Bicentenary of the Abolition of the Slave Trade, which focused attention on the City of Hull, the birthplace of William Wilberforce.

Religion and liberation are closely linked. The word 'Jubilee' comes from the ancient Hebrew tradition of setting aside every 50th year as a time of emancipation and restoration. Even the land was allowed to lie fallow, and the people, freed from bondage and exploitation, could go home and reclaim their own. Christians are promised that the Gospel truth will make them free; and the Eastern faiths seek Nirvana, release from the weary round of birth and death.

One name stands out poignantly in this record of the Jubilee programme: that of Father Anthony Storey, former Roman Catholic chaplain to Hull University and priest of Holy Cross Church, Cottingham, who had first addressed the Society in 1964. He it was who launched the series, giving the first lecture of the season. But, although he was expected to be an honoured guest at the anniversary dinner, he died on the First of May, nine days before the Annual Meeting. which opened with a silent tribute to his memory.

Although his sight was failing, Fr. Storey delivered the October lecture, *The Church – Hierarchy or Democracy?* with a clarity and vigour which would have done credit to a man half his age. 'Is authority a necessary evil?' he asked in a survey ranging from Aristotle to Karl Marx. Though we are drawn to the concept of equality and power-sharing, Platonic democracy does not work in practice. 'Order both falsifies – and preserves.'

Women bishops?

In a programme devoted to liberation, it was inevitable that the subject of women's rights and opportunities should be discussed, not least through the vexed question of ordination.

In November, when the Revd. Dr Charlotte Methuen arrived to address the Society on *The case for women bishops in the Church of England,* she came armed with a formidable list of dates from the mid-19th century to the present day, recording the progress of women towards ordination in the Anglican world. But, she pointed out, the idea of women bishops was not new: it had been there for most of the Church[1]s history. Evidence of feminine participation at the highest level went back to the time of the Apostles, as revealed in Paul's letters. In modern times, initiatives had come from the Far East in World War II, and America had given a lead with the election of Barbara Harris as Suffragan Bishop of Massachusetts in 1988. There was, however, a complex situation in England, with many ecumenical arguments to be resolved..

* * * *

Two days later, the Society joined Hull Branch of the Historical Association at the Danish Church to hear a talk by Ann Loades, Emerita Professor of Theology at the University of Durham, on *Josephine Butler – Campaigner for Women's Rights and Social Justice,* a detailed portrait of a remarkable protagonist in the cause of gender equality, and a fairer deal for the under-privileged generally.

Heritage

The loving, yet practical, work of women in healing the devastating social hurts created by rapid industrial change was also described by the

December speaker, Stephen Friend, Senior Lecturer in Theology at York St John University.

Examining *Religion and Identity in some North-East coast fishing communities,* he said that the best initiatives in coping with the problems came from women: They pioneered the re-educating, re-training and re--employment of the fishermen. They set up heritage centres, preserving the traditional crafts such as the gansey-patterns, which helped to identify dead men washed up or caught in trawler-nets. They made films, organised travelling exhibitions arid talks on family life, and recorded the many superstitions which grew up around this hard and hazardous way of life. There had been a dramatic decline in institutional religion in those communities. But that did not mean that people were less religious. 'Popular', 'folk', or 'lived' religion was often an attempt to make sense of the world we live in, but there was a huge overlap between the two.

Compassion

The custom of holding a Students' Evening gave place to a Members' Evening in January, when husband-and-wife duo Dr Alan Sheard and the Revd. Gillian Cooke Sheard took up the highly topical subject of *Homosexuality and Christianity in the 21st Century.* Both showed deep compassion and understanding in their approach to this controversial theme.

Dr Sheard, former Director of Public Health for East Yorkshire, dealt with the medical side, saying that 96% of men were heterosexual and 4% homosexual. This minority inherited the condition through the genes and chromosomes. It ran in families, a combination of genetic and environmental factors. Freud's theory that it could be caused by poor parental relationships had been discounted, along with 'getting into bad company' or being abused as a child. Change of sexual orientation was possible 'for anyone who makes the effort', but was extremely rare. There was an automatic reflex action between the body and the brain.

The Revd. Gillian, Anglican priest and chaplain to the Wolds Prison, called for a reappraisal of the scriptures in the light of scientific knowledge. Serious study was needed; sex was more complex than was originally thought. The Bible seemed to condemn homosexuality, but 'think about the developing views in cosmology and other subjects!' Sex was not just about procreation but also about companionship.

The two talks sparked some interesting discussion.

A matter of class

Professor Alistair Kee received a warm welcome when he returned to Hull University in February – despite the fact that he had been a somewhat controversial figure in his role as Senior Lecturer in Theology there during the 'seething sixties'. Unrepentant of his support for the students in the 'troubles' of that era, he declared that it was a pleasure to be back in the city.

Black Theology, he insisted, was a progression 'from slavery to class', having little to do with race or gender. He dismissed attempts to find condemnation of slavery in the Bible. In the Exodus story. the Israelites were freed from the Egyptians so that they might become 'slaves of God'. In the New Testament, Jesus becomes a captive and no-one tries to free him.

When Black Theology emerged in the 1960s, it bought with it 'much ideological baggage'. The end of Apartheid did not end the problem; race was not the problem but a symptom of another problem. The New Orleans floods brought further proof: those with the means escaped, those without did not – all a matter of social class!

No prude!

Did the conversion of Hull's greatest hero from a nominal Christian into a true believer and anti-slavery campaigner turn him into a humourless prude? Not according to Society president Dr David Bagchi when he delivered the March lecture, *Liberty, Equality. Fraternity and the Gospel in the Thought of William Wilberforce.*

The Emancipator remained a fun-loving fellow, an entertaining conversationalist and a clever mimic, though he always found something kind to say about those whose mannerisms he was lampooning.

The issue of the Abolition of the Slave Trade was not as straightforward as one might think. It might be assumed that Christians would accept that it was wrong to deprive people of their liberty, but acceptance of the practice was to be found in both Old and New Testaments, and scripture was used both to support and to attack the Slave Trade. Yet the balance of clerical voices seemed to be against the trade, and the outcome in 1807 left the victors crying, 'What can we abolish next?'

A challenge

For the penultimate meeting of the season, members moved to the Leslie Downs Theatre and returned to the subject of feminism.

The speaker was Dr Tina Beattie, Reader in Christian Studies at Roehampton University, and, though she is best known for her work on Marian Theology, on this occasion she turned to the topic of *Women, Religion and Human Rights,* which she felt presented 'a very deep challenge'.

Traditionally, religion gave man authority over woman, she said. 'Human Rights' was a 20th-century concept, following the Holocaust, and seeming to apply only to male citizens. In the modern world, a whole new language was needed to express 'Women's Rights', with compassion as its keynote. Naturally, the Roman Catholic Church's teaching on human reproduction raised many questions, and the evening ended with discussion on these controversial issues.

Full circle

And so at last we come full circle, to the climax of the celebrations, the Annual General Meeting, held in the University's Staff House at 7pm on 9 May 2007, fifty years to the day, and almost to the hour, of the inaugural meeting.

Good and bad fortune are entwined in the human condition. There were absent friends to be missed and remembered; but in so many ways we had reason to rejoice, and to be proud.

It was indeed fortunate that Dr Mary Tanner OBE had been able to accept the invitation to fulfil the key role of guest speaker. As a youthful member of the Theology Department's staff, specialising in Old Testament studies, Mary had taken on the post of secretary of the Society in 1962, continuing in office until 1965, when she was recruited for the committee. Since then she had scaled the heights of academic achievement, and it was as European President of the World Council of Churches that she returned to the city. This, as president David pointed out in his introduction, is the highest ecclesiastical rank that a laywoman may currently hold – other than that of Supreme Governor of the Church of England – the prerogative of the Queen! Slender and elegant, Mary delivered a masterly paper on *Ecumenism in the 21st Century,* covering the incredible strides towards unity and reconciliation achieved in recent years, but also emphasising the eggshell fragility of many of these rapprochements.

Afterwards, she was asked to provide a copy of her paper for wider circulation, and she readily agreed.

* * * *

The remainder of the AGM business had already been speedily dispatched, Treasurer Fiona Bagchi announcing a comfortable balance of £847.14.

The President proposed that Secretary Barbara Robinson be granted Honorary Membership in recognition of her work in recording the Society's history, and this was passed unanimously.

Then in the words of Lewis Carroll, it was 'all feasting and fun'. In its early days, the impecunious committee had been obliged to leave the suggestion of a Society dinner 'on the table', but by 2007 things had improved, and guests, including the Bishop of Hull, the Rt. Revd. Richard Frith, moved to the appropriately-named Jubilee Room for a veritable banquet!

The festivities concluded with one of those fortuitous little incidents which cannot be prearranged but which make the occasion special: Professor Lester Grabbe announced that, although he normally received a great many books in his department, mostly ordered from the publishers, one recent arrival really surprised him. It was a well-worn copy of *The Text of the Old Testament* by Ernst Würthwein, and was accompanied by a note from an anonymous 'old student' saying that his teacher, Dr Mary Tanner, had lent it to him when he was at the university. He asked if it could be returned to her, as he did not know her present whereabouts. Mary, who was a friend of the book's translator, Peter P. Ackroyd, was delighted, and told the company that she had spent hours searching for it.

That story makes the perfect ending to this story of the first half-century in the life of Hull and District Theological Society.

What of the future? That's another story . . .

PROGRAMME 2006-2007

Wednesday, 11 October, 2006
  Fr. Anthony Storey (sometime RC Chaplain to the University of Hull), *The Church –Hierarchy or Democracy?*

Tuesday, 28 November, 2006
  The Revd. & Hon. Dr Charlotte Methuen (Departmental Lecturer in Ecclesiastical History, University of Oxford), *The Case for Women Bishops in the Church of England.*

Thursday, 30 November, 2006
  Joint meeting with Hull Branch of the Historical Association at the Danish Church: Professor Ann Loades CBE, (Emerita Professor of Theology, University of Durham), *Josephine Butler – Campaigner for Women's Rights and Social Justice.*

Wednesday, 6 December, 2006
  Mr Stephen Friend (Senior Lecturer in Theology, York St John University) *Religion and Identity in some North-East coast fishing communities.*

Wednesday, 17 January, 2007
  Revd.Gillian Cooke and Dr Alan Sheard, *Homosexuality and Christianity in the 21st Century.*

Wednesday, 14 February, 2007
  Prof. Alistair Kee (Emeritus Professor of Religious Studies, University of Edinburgh; sometime Senior Lecturer in Theology, University of Hull), *Black Theology: A Lack of Class?*

Wednesday, 14 March, 2007
  The President, Dr David Bagchi, *Liberty, Equality, Fraternity, and the Gospel in the Thought of William Wilberforce.*

Wednesday, 18 April, 2007
  Dr Tina Beattie (Reader in Christian Studies, Roehampton University), *Women, Religion and Human Rights.*

Wednesday, 9 May, 2007
  7.00 pm Staff House University of Hull
  AGM AND JUBILEE DINNER
  Dr Mary Tanner OBE, (European President of the World Council of Churches; sometime Lecturer in Theology, University of Hull and Secretary of the Society), *Ecumenism for the 21st Century.*

Father Anthony Storey, one of the Society's most distinguished members, had many interests, among them Hull's link with Freetown, Sierra Leone, which he visited a number of times.

Here he is seen – raising a glass with Alfred Akibo-Betts, former Mayor of Freetown.

Celebrating the Golden Jubilee of Hull and District Theological Society (from left) Dr David Bagchi, President, Barbara Robinson, Secretary, Dr Mary Tanner OBE, guest speaker and one-time Society Secretary, and the Bishop of Hull, the Rt Revd. Richard Frith.

Officers on duty at the Society's 50th Annual General Meeting: Barbara Robinson, Secretary, Dr David Bagchi, President and Fiona Bagchi, Treasurer.

Guests assembling at Staff House for the 50th AGM and Jubilee Dinner.

Dr. Jackie Lukes in conversation with Father Gerard Burns, left, and the Revd. Stephen Deas.

Index

Abramson, Dr Edward, 69
Ackroyd, Revd. Prof. Peter, 37
Akibo-Betts, Alfred, Mayor of Freetown, Liberia, *108*
Alexander, Dr (later Prof.) Loveday, 74, 75, 99, 102
Ambler, Dr R.W., 57
Anderson, Dominic, 52, 55, 57
Anderson, G.W., 18
Andrew, Dr Richard, 96, 98
Andrews, Dr K.W., 29
Armstrong, Prof. A.M., 34
Asad, Talal, 34
Atherton, Canon Dr John, 62, 65
Atkinson, Revd. David, 51, 54
Atkinson, Revd. (later Canon) Dr (later Prof.) James, 10, 15, 17, 18, 20, 23, 25, 26, 28, 31, 39, 51
Atkinson, Philip, 39, 40
Aujla, Dr, first Guru Nanak Memorial Lecturer, 36, 37
Baelz, Very Revd. Peter, 46, 48
Bagchi, Dr David, President 1997-, *viii*, 62, 69, 71, 73-7 *passim*, 80, 83-9 *passim*, 91, 93, 94, 96, 97, 98, 101, 102, 105, 106, 107, *109*
Bagchi, Fiona, 82, 85, 87, 88, 93, 97, 101, 106, *109*
Baker, Revd. Dr Frank, 10, 11, 17, 18, 19
Bamford, Dr T.W., 40
Bannister, Revd. G.A., 23, 24
Barclay, Revd., 21
Barclay, Prof. John, 95, 98
Barnard, Revd. L.W., 36
Barr, Revd. Prof. James, 51, 52, 57, 59
Barrett, Revd. Dr (later Prof.) C.K., 19, 30, 52
Barry, Jonathan, 40
Barry, Dom Patrick, 53
Bash, Revd. Dr Anthony, 79, 81, 93
Baslington, E., 27, 30, 31, 34, 36, 38
Batchelor, Mr., 18
Batstone, Patricia, 41
Beattie, Dr Tina, 105, 107
Beauchamp, Gerald, 45
Becker, Revd. Gerhard, 63
Bell, Revd. G.R., 26, 28
Bentall, Mary, 55
Bergmark, Pastor I., 21, 25
Bernasconi, John C., 47, 49, 64, 66
Betts, J., 47
Bhattacharji, Dr Santha, 89
Bickersteth, Dr J. Elfride, 35, 36, 49, 51, 55, 64, 66, 76, 77, 88, 91, 97

Biggar, Prof. Nigel, 89, 92
Biggs, Dr John, 29, 41, 42, 61
Billingham, I.R., Founder Treasurer, 10, 15, 20
Billington, Dr Louis, 46, 48, 65
Binfield, Dr Clyde, 66
Blanch, Most Revd. Stuart, Archbishop of York, 47-50 *passim*
Blanchard, H.W., 18, 21
Bloom, Archbishop Anthony, Metropolitan of Sourozh, 35
Boaden, Miss M., 27
Bouquet, A.C., 21
Bowman, Leslie, 51
Boyce-Tillman, Dr June, 75, 79
Bradley, Dr Ian, 101-2
Bradley, S.A.J., 65
Bradshaw, Dr John, 69
Brain, Patrick, 37
Brett, Prof. R.L., 11, 15, 17
Bridge, C.D., 10, 19, 28
Briggs, Dr J., 29
Bright, Father Laurence, O.P., 31, 32
Broadbent, Ann, 83
Brooks, Dr Peter, 28
Brown, Revd. Malcolm, 69
Brown, Revd. Dr R., 51
Brown, Rosa, 81, 88, 89, 91
Bruce, A.J., 36
Bruce, Prof. F.F., 20, 35
Burkitt, Revd. Paul, 90, 92
Burns, Father Gerard, *110*
Burt, Revd. G.M., 25, 26, 27, 28
Buss, Revd Michael, 44, 45
Calvert, Revd. G.A., 58
Campbell, Dr W.S., 57
Cant, Revd. Chancellor R.L., 17
Capern, Dr Amanda, 96, 98
Carby-Hall, Dr Hillary, 64
Carr, Dr, Stephen, 67
Carroll, Revd. J.V., SM, 26, 27
Carrotte, Ruth, 40
Carter, Revd. D., 20, 23, 25, 26, 28, 30, 34
Casey, Dr P.M., 54
Cassidy, Father Patrick, 11
Castle, Prof., 20, 21
Caygill, Geoff, 66
Caygill, Lorna, 62
Chadwick, Very Revd. Dr Henry, 52
Charlton, Dr D.G., 20, 24
Cherry, David, 44
Christie, Revd. G., 18, 21
Clark, Heather, 86, 89
Clements, Revd. R.E., 41

111

Clines, D.J.A., 50
Clines, Revd. Jeremy, 100, 102
Clithero, Miss S., 34
Cockman, Paul, 58
Coggan, Dr Donald, Archbishop of York, 23, 27
Cole, Revd. R.L., 19
Collis, Ruth, 42
Cook, Christopher, 45
Cooke, Revd. Gillian, *see* Sheard, Revd. Gillian Cooke
Cooper, Dr Chaim J., 22, 23, 25, 33, 34
Coote, Revd. David, 88, 97, 101
Coote, Dr Lesley, 90, 92
Cox, C.B., 19
Cragg, Bishop Kenneth, 45
Crouch, Revd. Prof. David, 95, 97
Culling, Revd. Dr Elizabeth, 70
Daly, Revd. Father Gabriel, 43
Darroch, Revd. R.H., 38, 39
David, Revd. Prof. Charles, 31, 32
Davies, Miss A.L., 41
Davies, Revd. Dr (later Prof.) J.G., 20, 21, 25
Davies, Dr John C., 61
Davies, Prof. P.R., 87, 89
Davies, Revd. R.E., 29
Davis, Revd. Charles, 31
Day, John, 51, 52
Dean, Revd. J.M.B., 20, 23, 25
Dearey, Paul, 80, 81, 93, 94
Deas, Revd. Canon L. Stephen, 76, 77, 88, 97, 101, *110*
Dermott, D., 30, 31
Dickason, John, 39
Dickens, Prof. A.G., 11, 15, 17, 51
Dillistone, Dr F.W., 14
Dodd, Dr (later Prof.) C.H., 5, 46, 48, 50
Dodd, Sara, 60, 61
Dodd, Dr Tony, 89
Dominian, Dr Jack, 54
Donald, Josephina, 91
Douie, Dr Decima L., 20
Doyle, Pat, 86, 89
Duffy, Prof. Eamon, 6, 33, 34, 49, 50, 56
Dugard, Revd. Donald, 38, 40
Dunkley, Miss A.R., 41
Dunn, Dr (later Prof.) James, 45, 67
Dyson, Revd. Prof. A.G., 63
Earl, Prof. Donald, 53
Easton, Dr Malcolm F., 18, 19, 35
Eccleston, Ann, 36, 38, 51, 55, 57, 86, 89, 91, 97, 101
Ellingworth, Dr Paul, 58
Elliott, Dr J. Keith, 61, 63, 84

Ellis, Revd. Ieuan P., President 1983-7, *vi*, 7, 30, 31, 44, 47, 49, 54
Ellis, J.T., 15
Ernst, Revd. Cornelius, O.P., 29
Evans, Revd. Prof. C.E., 21
Farmer, Prof. H.H., 18
Farr, Heather M., 39, 41
Farrar, Dr Austin, 15-16
Fenney, L., 15, 26, 27
Fitzpatrick, Dr P.J., 42
Flood, Margaret M. (formerly Henson), 47, 49, 52, 55, 57
Ford, Prof. Alan, 85
Forster, Dr Peter, 61
Foster, Revd. D.W., 19
Francis, Revd. Tegwyn, 36, 37
Freeman, Clifford B., 20, 21, 23, 25, 26, 27, 36, 37, 44
Frend, Prof. W.H.C., 39
Friend, Stephen, 104, 107
Frith, Rt. Revd. Richard, Bishop of Hull, 86, 89, 106, *109*
Fudge, Prof. Erik C., 42, 58
Fussell, Miss M., 22, 25
Ganney, Revd. Rachel, 99, 102
Garner, Revd. Rod, 67
Gelston, Revd. A., 31
George, Revd. A. Raymond, 21, 25
Gibson, Peter, 86, 87, 89
Gill, R., 28, 30
Gilley, Dr Sheridan, 55
Ginther, Dr James, 85
Glebe-Møller, Prof. Jens, 93, 94
Goldsmith, Brig. A., 20, 22
Gordon-Kerr, Canon Dr Francis, 62
Gosling, Dr D.L., 45
Goulder, (now Revd.) Catherine ('Kate'), 38, 41, 44, 45, 47, 49
Goulder, Dr M.D, 49, 57, 58
Grabbe, Prof. Lester L., President 1991-3, *viii*, 52, 54, 55, 57, 61, 64, 85,-9 *passim*, 93, 94, 95, 97, 98, 106
Graham, Dr Elaine, 65, 69
Greenslade, Revd. Canon S.L., 19
Griffiths, Dom Ambrose, 53
Guilding, Prof. Aileen, 20, 21, 22, 25
Habgood, Most Revd. Dr John, Archbishop of York, 51, 56, 58, 67, 69
Haddon, Dr Wilmer, 63, 65
Haines, M.R., 38
Hall, Dr John, 62
Hammond, Revd. P., 27
Hanson, Revd. Prof. Anthony T., President 1962-82, *vi*, 24, 28, 29, 46, 49, 55
Hanson, Revd. (later Rt Revd) Dr (later Prof.) Richard P.C., 16, 17, 29, 37, 41, 42, 49, 50

Harris, Augustine, Bishop of Middlesbrough, 46, 48
Harrison, Dr Carol, 67-8, 69
Harrison, Jean, 62
Harrison, Kevin, 36, 38, 40
Harry, Miss P.M., 31
Haseldine, Dr Julian, 90, 92
Hastings, Prof. Adrian, 63
Hazlett, Dr Ian, 89, 92
Healey, Dr John F., 65
Heaton, Very Revd. Eric, 42
Hellenic Association, 33
Hennell, Revd. Canon Michael M., 49, 50
Hensell, Christine, 55
Henson, Margaret M., *see* Flood, Margaret
Herbert, Revd. Prof. A.S., 27
Hicks, W.T., 31, 34
Higgins, A.G.B., 20
Higginson, June, 53, 55, 57, 63
Historical Association, 5, 16, 17, 33, 103
Hodgson, Mr., 61
Hodgson, Karen, 51
Holland, Glyn, 48
Hollenweger, Prof. W., 51
Holroyd, Kerry, 31, 36, 37
Hooke, Prof. S.H., 18, 19
Hooker, Prof. Morna D., 30, 53, 69, 93, 94
Hoose, Dr Bernard, 80, 81
Hope, Most Revd. Dr David, Archbishop of York, 69, 86, 87, 88, 89
Hughes, Dr David, 80, 81
Hughes, M.M., 52
Hull and District Theological Society, founded 1-5; programmes, 5-6, 51; presidents, *v-viii*, 7; first committee meeting, 10; rules, 12-13, 27, 78-9; first public meeting, 14; first annual general meeting, 14-15; first Guru Nanak Memorial Lecture, 36, 37; joint meetings with the Hellenic Association 33, with the Historical Association, 33, with Hull Classical Association, 33, 34, 35, 84, with the Newman Circle, 29, 31, 32, 33, 35, with the Religious Education Association, 48, with the University Theological Association, 32, 33, 48; women in, 45; and celebration's of Martin Luther's birth, 51; suspends activities 1997, 71-4; relaunches 1998, 74; newsletter *Theologia*, 80, 82, 84, 86, 89, 92-3, 96, 101; website, 80, 83; publication of *Hull Theological Papers* begins, 80, 83
Hull, Bishop of, 17, 18, 35, 86, 89, 106, *109*
Hull Classical Association, 33, 34, 35, 84, 87
Hull Daily Mail, 16, 24, 33, 84
Hull, John M., 59
Hull Municipal Training College, 7, 11, 19

Hulmes, Edward, 41
Humberside Association for Religious and Moral Education, 62
Hume, Rt Revd. Dom Basil, O.S.B., 37
Hunter, Revd. F.G., 34, 38
Huston, Mary, 48
Igwara, Dr Obi, 88
James, John, 62
Jarret-Kerr, Father Martin, 42
jasper, Revd. Dr David, 46-7, 63
Jasper, Very Revd. Ronald, 45
Jenkins, Revd. Prof. David, 47-8
Jessop, Prof. Thomas Edmund, 4, 15, 19, 20, 23
Johnston, Duncan, 52
Jones, Prof. D.A., 41
Jones, Revd. Jim, 74, 79
Jones, Prof. Kathleen, 39
Kay, Dr A., 21
Kay, Miss M., 31
Kearney, Mary Rose, 76, 77, 88, 94, 97, 101
Kee, Dr (later Prof.) Alistair A., 37, 53, 104-5, 107
Kennedy, David, 41, 43
Keron, Jennifer C., 33, 34
King, Dr Ursula, 53, 54
Kjaergaard, Revd. Hjørdis, 93
Knott, Dr Kim, 62
Køhn, Dr Rosemary, 93, 94
Lampe, Revd. Prof. G.W.H., 30
Langdon, Revd. E., 41, 44
Large, Dr Peter, 70
Lash, Prof. N.L.A., 48
Last, Miss H.M., 44
Lawton, Clive, 62
Leaney, Revd. A.R.C., 18, 27
Lessing, G.E., 58
Lewis, Bob, 47
Lewis, Graham, 45
Lewis, Prof. H.D., 39
Lewis, Dr Philip, 80, 85
Lieu, Dr Judith, 55
Lieu, Dr Samuel, 53
Lindars, Revd. Prof. Barnabas, 47, 53
Ling, Prof. Trevor, 41
Little, Dr Edmund, 50
Loades, Dr (later Prof.) Ann, 66, 103, 107
Loughlin, Revd. Gordon O., 36, 38
Louth, Revd. Andrew, 61
Lukes, Dr Jackie, *110*
Lyons, Frank, 44, 46, 47, 49, 55, 57, 64, 66, 68
Lyons, J., 38
McClelland, Prof. V. Alan, 45, 100, 102
McDowall, Revd. Robin, 101
McFadyen, Dr Alistair, 69
McKay, Prof. D.M., 40

113

McKay, Revd. Dr J.W., 38, 39
Mackey, Prof. J.P., 46, 48
MacMahon, Mrs K.A., 10, 19
McPherson, Revd. Ian N., 29, 30
Macquarrie, Revd. Prof. John, 6, 45
Macquiban, Prof. Tim, 90, 92
McSweeney, B., 50
Malalasekera, Prof. G.P., 31
Maltby, Dr Judith, 79, 81
Manson, Prof. William, 16
Marchant, Robert, 39
Mariau, Dr Daniel, 48, 83, 90-1, 92, 94
Mariau, Vivienne, 83
Mathew, Revd. Gervasse, O.P., 18, 21
Mathews, Dr H.F., 35
Maunder, Dr Chris, 95, 97
Mayfield, Prof. G.E.T., 3, 14-15, 21
Meeres, Dr J., 29
Methuen, Revd. Dr Charlotte, 103, 107
Michie, Dr A.J., 37
Miles, Dr Graham, 62
Mill, John Stuart, 54
Milligan, A., 47
Möller, Prof. B., 51
Moloney, Prof. Brian, 54, 70
Moltmann, Jürgen, 99
Monti, Prof. Anthony, 92, 94
More, Michael, 42
Morgan, Revd. Dr Teresa, 101
Morris, Sister Alexia, 41, 44
Moulton, Revd. H., 28
Music Society, 20
Myhill, Revd. F., 44, 49, 51
Naismith, Alexandra, 37
Newman Circle, 20, 21, 29, 31, 32, 33, 35
Niblett, Prof. W.R., 21, 22, 25
Nicholson, Very Revd. Ernest, 43
Nineham, Prof. Dennis, 6, 18
Nixon, Revd. R.E., 19
Norman, Prof. A.F., 40
North, Dr J. Lionel, President 1993-7, *vii*, 33, 49, 50, 51, 54, 55, 57, 59, 64, 66, 68, 76, 82, 86, 95
North, Dr Wendy Sproston, President 1987-91, *vii*, 41, 43, 46, 47, 49, 55, 57, 60, 76, 82, 83, 86, 95
O'Brien, Rt Revd. K., 50
O'Riordan, Prof. Sean, C.S.S.R., 36
Ortiz, Gaye, 85
Overell, Anne, 85
Page, Edgar, 59
Palliser, Prof. David, 66, 67
Parker, Dr David, 63
Parker, Jonathan, 46, 48, 83
Parker, Revd. Dr T.H.L., 32
Parkin, Dr Harry, 55
Parrinder, Prof. Geoffrey, 39

Parsons, Dr Susan, 67
Pasolini, Pier Paolo, his film *The Gospel according to St. Matthew*, 36, 37
Paterson, Dr Ronald, 45
Payne, Revd. Alan, 65
Pearson, Prof. David B., 65
Pepper, Revd. L.R., 41, 42
Percy, Revd. Canon Dr Martyn, 80, 81
Pike, David, 37
Pinthus, Eva I., 28, 42
Pollard, Prof. Arthur, 35
Pond, Prof. D.A., 42
Poore, Revd. Jim, 67
Porteous, Prof. N.W., 20
Price, Colin M., 38, 40
Priestman, M., 46
Proctor, Dr, 25
Purvis, Anthony, 45
Pye, Prof. Michael, 52
Pyper, Dr Hugh, 86, 89
Quinn, Revd. A.H.R., 30, 31
Rajapikse, Sir Lalita, High Commissioner for Ceylon, 33, 34
Ramsay, Rt. Revd. Ian, Bishop of Durham, 39
Ramsey, Dr Michael, Archbishop of York, 15, 17, 23, 41, 43
Reece, Prof., 20, 21
Reid, Revd. Prof. J.K.S., 21
Religious Education Association, 48
Richard, Sister Mary, 31, 38
Richards, Linda, 76, 77, 81, 82, 85, 87, 88, 91, 97, 101
Richardson, Very Revd. Dr Alan, 34
Richardson, Revd. W., 18, 21
Rigby, Revd. Philip, 44, 46
Ring, Maura, 42
Ritmeyer, Dr L., 65
Robertson, Alec, 20, 23
Robinson, Barbara, 75, 76, 80, 81, 88, 94, 97, 101, 106, *109*
Robinson, Bishop John, 6
Rogerson, Revd. (later Prof.) John W., 40, 58
Rowe, Revd. Trevor T., 10-11, 13, 15, 20
Rowley, Revd. Prof. H.H., 17
Rupp, Revd. Dr (later Prof.) E. Gordon, 18, 23
Russell, Revd. Dr David S., 51
Ryder, Dr T.T.B., 61
Rye, Mark, 40
Sanders, Revd. J.N., 20, 23
Sanders, Dr Valerie, 62
Sawyer, Dr J.F.A., 48
Schaar, Pastor E.H., 31, 32
Schnackenburg, Prof. Rudolph, 40
Schnellbächer, Pastor E.L., 39, 40

Secret, Judith, 38, 39, 41
Sedgwick, Dr Peter, 61, 63
Sedgwick, Revd. Peter, 65, 69
Sen, A.K., 30
Sentamu, Dr John, Archbishop of York, 99
Sewell, E.J., 11, 17-20 *passim*, 22
Shakespeare, Dr Steven, 86, 88
Shanks, Revd. Canon Andrew, 96-7, 98
Sharps, Geoffrey, 91
Shaw, Taylor, 33
Sheard, Dr Alan, 104, 107
Sheard, Revd. Gillian Cooke, 104, 107
Shorter, Mrs J., see Shorter, Mary
Shorter, Mary, 22, 23, 25, 26, 34
Silverwood, Trevor, 91
Simon, Revd. Dr Ulrich E., 23
Skemp, Prof. J.B., 37
Smart, Prof. R. Ninian, 26, 46, 47
Smith, Revd. Michael, 44, 46
Solhdoost, Sister Kira, 41, 42
Sonderbø, Dr Susanne, 93, 94
Sproston, Wendy, *see* North, Wendy Sproston
Sproxton, Revd. Vernon, 40
Stanbridge, Revd. L.C., 15, 17, 18, 20, 23, 24, 25, 28
Stern, Dr Julian, 90, 92
Stevenson, Revd. Canon S., 23, 24
Stobart, Miss P.A., 36
Stonehouse, Miss, 22
Storey, Father Anthony J., 28, 35, 39, 49, 54, 103, 107, *108*
Stubley, Revd. Dr Peter D., 55, 57, 64, 66, 67, 68, 70
Sturman, Revd. Geoffrey, 51
Sutton, Jenny, 53
Swinburne, Miss M., 28, 29
Swinburne, R.G., 29
Sykes, Very Revd. Dr Norman, 17, 20
Sykes, Prof. Stephen, 55
Symes, Wendy, 42
Tanner, Mrs J.B, *see* Tanner, Dr Mary, O.B.E
Tanner, Dr Mary O.B.E, 24-5, 26, 27, 29, 31, 106-7, *109*
Taylor, Dr P.A.M., 36
Telford, Revd. Dr William, 69
Thewlis, Dr J.C., 42
Thieme, Revd. P., 18, 21
Thomas, Revd. J. Heywood, 21, 25
Thomas, Prof. L.H.C., 41, 42
Thompson, Dr B.P., 58
Thompson, Matthew, 53
Thompson, Revd. Patrick J., 10, 11, 12, 15, 17, 18, 20, 23, 25, 26, 27, 44
Thrall, Dr Margaret E., 50
Tillich, Paul, 3
Tinker, Revd. Melvin, 89

Tinsley, Revd. E.J. (later Bishop of Bristol), Founder President, *v*, 10, 16, 20, 22, 24, 27, 28, 40
Todd, Dr Helena, 11
Todd, John M., 37
Torrance, J.F., 21
Toy, Revd. Canon Dr John, 70
Tree, Susanne, 44, 46, 48
Tucker, Revd. K.R., 21, 22, 25, 26
Tustin, Rt. Revd. Dr David, Bishop of Grimsby, 75, 79, 80, 83
Tweedy, Revd. Mark, C.R., 18, 21
Tyagi, R.C., 30
University of Hull, 1-2, 3-4, 10, 19, 20, 22, 24, 28-9, 30, 31, 32, 33, 35, 48, 55, 56, 59-60, 64, 65, 66, 67, 69, 70, 71, 73, 77, 80-4 *passim*, 86-94 *passim*, 97-8; Theological Society, 28, 30, 32, 33, 48; Theology Day Schools, 56, 61, 63-7 *passim*, 69, 70, 71, 73, 81, 86-8 *passim*, 90-4 *passim*, 97-8
Vardy, Dr Peter, 76
Vaughan, Revd. Patrick, 45
Verity, John, 38, 39
Vesey, Canon N.A., 10
Vincent, Revd. John J., 37
Wakefield, Revd. G.S., 27
Walker, D., 30, 31
Walker, Revd. G.S.M., 29
Walker, Revd. S., 21, 25
Walton, Prof. Robert C., 65
Wansbrough, Dom Henry, 45
Ward, Rt Revd. Dr J.W.C., Bishop of London, 19
Ward, Judith, 86, 88
Ward, Revd. Rodney, 76, 77, 81, 83, 86, 88
Wardlow, Michael, 62
Wasserstein, Prof. A., 33
Watt, Dr John A., 34
Watts, Ian, 52
Weinberger, Dr Joanna, 58
Wells, Revd. Adrian J., 55, 57, 64
Werner, Pastor C.O.H., 19, 21
Werrell, Revd. Ralph, 80, 81
West, Revd. H.C., 31, 32
Westwood, Bishop Bill, 80
Whatling, Marion, 39
White, Dr Gavin, 90, 92
Whitehouse, Revd. W.A., 18, 20, 23
Whittle, R.A., 20, 22
Whybray, Revd. Dr (later Prof.) R.Norman, 31, 35, 38, 48, 52, 53, 54, 64, 65
Wijngaards, Revd. Dr Hans, 45
Wilcox, Prof. Max, 55
Wilde, John, 43
Wilkinson, Heward, 37
Wilkinson, Keith, 34, 36
William Temple Association, 5, 8